News Agencies

This book explores the role of international news agencies and investigates whether they have been able to adapt to the contemporary media landscape following the disruption wrought by fake news, social media and an increasingly polarised public discourse.

News Agencies addresses the key players in the industry, beginning with the "big three" (Reuters, The Associated Press and Agence France-Presse) and then moving on to the newest global player, Bloomberg. It also explores the role of alternative providers of international news which are seeking to challenge the Western-centric perspective of the agencies. Drawing on interviews with senior editors, Stephen Jukes investigates the challenges agencies face in terms of their editorial strategy and business models in today's social media context. At a time when there is widespread distrust in the media and agencies are relying increasingly on user-generated content as a source for news, Jukes critically explores the role of these agencies in the debate over fake news and policies on objectivity, impartiality and verification.

Shedding light on a sector of the news industry that has steadfastly remained out of the public spotlight, this book will be of interest to students and academics in the fields of journalism and media studies.

Stephen Jukes is an Emeritus Professor in the Faculty of Media and Communication at Bournemouth University. He worked in Europe, the Middle East and the Americas as a Foreign Correspondent, Regional Editor and Global Head of News at the international news agency Reuters before moving into the academic world in 2005. His research focuses on areas of objectivity and emotion in news with an emphasis on conflict journalism and trauma. He is a trustee of the Dart Centre for Journalism & Trauma in Europe and of the Institute for War & Peace Reporting.

Disruptions: Studies in Digital Journalism
Series editor: Bob Franklin

Disruptions refers to the radical changes provoked by the affordances of digital technologies that occur at a pace and on a scale that disrupts settled understandings and traditional ways of creating value, interacting and communicating both socially and professionally. The consequences for digital journalism involve far reaching changes to business models, professional practices, roles, ethics, products and even challenges to the accepted definitions and understandings of journalism. For Digital Journalism Studies, the field of academic inquiry which explores and examines digital journalism, disruption results in paradigmatic and tectonic shifts in scholarly concerns. It prompts reconsideration of research methods, theoretical analyses and responses (oppositional and consensual) to such changes, which have been described as being akin to 'a moment of mind-blowing uncertainty'.

Routledge's book series, *Disruptions: Studies in Digital Journalism*, seeks to capture, examine and analyse these moments of exciting and explosive professional and scholarly innovation which characterize developments in the day-to-day practice of journalism in an age of digital media, and which are articulated in the newly emerging academic discipline of Digital Journalism Studies.

Newsrooms and the Disruption of the Internet
A Short History of Disruptive Technologies, 1990–2010
Will Mari

News Agencies
Anachronism or Lifeblood of the Media System?
Stephen Jukes

For more information about this series, please visit: www.routledge.com/Disruptions/book-series/DISRUPTDIGJOUR

News Agencies
Anachronism or Lifeblood of the Media System?

Stephen Jukes

LONDON AND NEW YORK

First published 2022
by Routledge
4 Park Square, Milton Park, Abingdon, Oxon OX14 4RN

and by Routledge
605 Third Avenue, New York, NY 10158

Routledge is an imprint of the Taylor & Francis Group, an informa business

© 2022 Stephen Jukes

The right of Stephen Jukes to be identified as author of this work has been asserted in accordance with sections 77 and 78 of the Copyright, Designs and Patents Act 1988.

All rights reserved. No part of this book may be reprinted or reproduced or utilised in any form or by any electronic, mechanical, or other means, now known or hereafter invented, including photocopying and recording, or in any information storage or retrieval system, without permission in writing from the publishers.

Trademark notice: Product or corporate names may be trademarks or registered trademarks, and are used only for identification and explanation without intent to infringe.

British Library Cataloguing-in-Publication Data
A catalogue record for this book is available from the British Library

Library of Congress Cataloging-in-Publication Data
A catalog record has been requested for this book

ISBN: 978-0-367-46905-4 (hbk)
ISBN: 978-1-032-25855-3 (pbk)
ISBN: 978-1-003-02965-6 (ebk)

DOI: 10.4324/9781003029656

Typeset in Times New Roman
by KnowledgeWorks Global Ltd.

To Yvonne, Dominic and Timothy

Contents

Acknowledgements   x

Introduction: News agencies – a world unto themselves   1
Introduction 1
Breaking news from faraway places 2
A rich history of scoops 4
Chapter overview 9
Notes 12
References 13

1 From carrier pigeons to social media   15
Introduction 15
Birth of the agencies 16
Establishing news values and norms 18
Competition and the Agency Alliance Treaty 20
Breaking free of government shackles 21
Translating independence into a style and ethos 25
UNESCO and the charge of imperialism 26
Corporate change and the building blocks of today's agency landscape 27
The competition for dominance 29
Conclusion: How the wheels came off 34
Notes 35
References 36

2 Weathering the storm: Can more than 150 years of tradition save the news agencies? 39

Introduction 39
A continual slide in earnings but is there a route to recovery? 41
Adapting to social media and the rush to digital 45
Editorial is the target for cost cutting 49
Who wants plain vanilla news? 54
Conclusion 56
Notes 57
References 58

3 Back to the future: Social media, fact-checking and plain vanilla journalism 59

Introduction 59
Fact-checking takes on new dimensions 60
Fact-checking in practice 64
Still gatekeeping or "gatewatching"? 67
The danger within 72
Covering Trump 76
Conclusion 78
Notes 80
References 81

4 Collaboration, community and state actors 84

Introduction 84
Taking a different approach 86
Breaking the taboo about collaboration 88
A community-based approach 93
Do the soft power players change anything? 97
Conclusion 100
Notes 102
References 104

Conclusion: News agencies – rooted in the past and looking to the future 106

Introduction 106
The last outpost 108
Digging in for the long haul 110
The pitfalls of social media 112
Going back to their roots 113
Notes 116
References 116

Index 118

Acknowledgements

When Bob Franklin, the series editor of *Disruptions*, asked me to write a book about the world's news agencies I was both delighted and filled with trepidation. I had worked for Reuters for well over 20 years, had lived and breathed its culture and, as I moved into more senior editorial positions, witnessed the inner workings of the organisation at first hand. Clearly, with a further 15 years of experience in the academic world after leaving Reuters, the request made absolute sense. Two years on, having negotiated the disruptions to academic life wrought by COVID-19, I can only hope that I have done Bob Franklin and the series justice. I have been constantly aware that there are journalists at Reuters who covered far more important stories than I ever did. And it is difficult to write about an organisation which for so many years dominated my working life and remain objective – ironically one of the watchwords of news agency journalism. I have done my best to produce a balanced and useful analysis of the global news agencies, conscious that the likes of AP, AFP and Bloomberg were, in agency speak, "the opposition" and that I had much to learn about them. I would therefore like to thank and acknowledge all those journalists who took time to speak with me, often on a background basis, sometimes on the record, as I researched the book. I had forgotten how sensitive the business of news is and hope I have been critical yet fair in my analysis. My thanks also go to my long-suffering family, my wife Yvonne and sons Dominic and Timothy who have had to put up with interrupted holidays and the constant refrain "I'm working on the book." My thanks go as well to the publishing team at Routledge for their support, including Elizabeth Cox and Priscille Biehlmann plus, of course, the series editor Bob Franklin. This was never designed as a book that "dishes the dirt" on the agencies or relates an untold inside story. Instead it seeks to present a critical yet balanced analysis of the challenges and threats they face in a world of fake news, disinformation and conspiracy theories. I passionately believe in the power of journalism to cut through this mire, verify the truth and, as the cliché goes, hold power to account. Long may the news agencies continue to perform this role.

Introduction

News agencies – a world unto themselves

Flash: a news alert of transcendent importance, consisting of a few words and followed immediately by a publishable bulletin series. Very few flashes have been sent by AP; two were sent within two hours, however, on 9/11 – one when each tower fell – Associated Press Glossary of Wire Service terms, 2007.

Introduction

Every industry has its own language, often impenetrable to outsiders. Journalism is no exception and nowhere is this more pronounced than in the world of international news agencies. The Associated Press even has a helpful glossary to explain its terms to the uninitiated. Certainly, when I first climbed the stairs of 85 Fleet Street and joined Reuters in London as a young reporter from provincial newspapers four decades ago, the newsroom was a baffling experience. What was the difference between a "flash," a "bulletin" and an "alert"? Just how many bells did each of these brief messages of breaking news need? What was the difference between a "Nightlead" and a "1st lead" (or lede)? And what exactly did the World Desk do?

I learnt, of course, within days and soon was living and breathing a very special culture that binds "wire" journalists together. It was the start of a more than 20-year career as a foreign correspondent at Reuters that took me all over the world, from Cold War Europe, to the Middle East and, as an editor, to the Americas. That special culture in the Lutyens headquarters of Reuters,[1] at a time when newspapers still ruled the roost in Fleet Street, certainly had its quirks. The whole of the World Desk, the main editing hub of the breaking news operation, would stop each morning when the tea trolley arrived on the floor. Hard-nosed hacks would form a polite queue for a tea and bun. Later in the day, (not always much later) various drinking establishments

DOI: 10.4324/9781003029656-1

would be visited, not least one called Mrs Moon's further up Fleet Street. As the late, legendary Reuters journalist George Short wrote when Mrs Moon's closed its doors in 1984, it was a shabby dive bar "with a near-legendary mystique that often puzzled the uninitiated." I would discover that other newsrooms in other cities around the world had their own cultural peculiarities but the underlying ethos was deadly serious and always the same: be first with the news. Get it right and stick to the facts. Seconds matter, not minutes.

That is still the ethos today but somehow the media world has become infinitely more complicated than it seemed to me during my early years at Reuters. This is not a book about my reminiscences as a journalist but rather an attempt to shed light on the role of news agencies in today's rapidly changing media landscape; they are virtually unknown to the general public and equally are barely discussed in academic literature. The chapters that follow are, however, certainly informed by my practice and insights into the editorial and strategic management of one major international news agency garnered as I rose through the ranks. Not least, in my final years, I was the senior journalist responsible for upholding what to this day are known as Reuters "Trust Principles," established at the height of World War II in 1941 and designed to ensure that the news agency and its employees act at all times with integrity, independence, and freedom from bias. Those trust principles go to the very heart of the news agency ethos.

Breaking news from faraway places

Each of today's "big three" international news agencies, Reuters, the Associated Press (AP) and Agence France-Presse (AFP), can trace their roots back to the middle of the 19th century. In 2021, AP celebrated the 175th anniversary of its founding. As the agencies became established, so they played a key role in developing many of the values and norms of today's journalism, not least the so-called objectivity paradigm which will be discussed, together with the controversy surrounding it, later in this book. To the three major agencies, can be added Bloomberg News,[2] born out of the financial boom in 1990 and today the biggest competitor to Reuters in financial news. Each of them can count about 2,500 journalists worldwide and claim to have extensive global reach. AP states that one way or another more than half the world's population sees its journalism every day; Reuters says its news is read and seen by more than one billion people worldwide every day, including more than 750 television broadcasters in 115 countries.

The agencies have until most recently operated almost entirely in a wholesale, or business-to-business market for news, pictures and video, where their clients are other news organisations. In addition, agencies like Reuters and Bloomberg can rely on financial institutions worldwide to subscribe to their news services, knowing full well that breaking news often has an immediate impact on market prices, whether that be the value of shares, bonds, foreign exchange, commodities or more arcane financial instruments. As such, it has become a highly profitable source of business for Reuters and Bloomberg. As Michael Palmer observes in his history of international news agencies, general news may be valuable to society but it is rarely profitable (2019: 243):

> Ever-changing, fast-moving financial and commercial news makes agencies money; political and general news rarely does so.

By combining their newsfeeds with trading platforms, yield calculations and analytics, these two agencies have become an integral component of today's financial markets where a "beat" is measured in seconds (and can yield profits to a trader who can be first to react). In fact, as will be examined later in Chapter 1, Reuters shift of emphasis in the late 1970s towards coverage of specialist financial news at the expense of traditional "general news" led to widespread resentment among older news hands and initially general and financial news were housed on different floors of the 85 Fleet Street head office (Bartram, 2003: 389). Today, Reuters and Bloomberg have the power to influence financial markets within seconds through their news feeds as central banks move interest rates up and down, companies announce earnings or Middle East tensions spark unrest in the global oil markets. Given this market sensitivity, the performance of their journalists is measured not in minutes but in seconds. News of a central bank interest rate change "flashed" 10 seconds behind the "opposition" is little short of a catastrophe and, in my experience, always led to an uncomfortable "post mortem" investigation.

Such breaking news is, of course, the bread and butter of agency journalism but so too is the myth and romance of the foreign correspondent. The British novelist Evelyn Waugh delivered a lasting depiction of the foreign correspondent in his 1938 novel *Scoop*, dramatising the adventures of the hapless William Boot, complete with his "cleft sticks."[3] Certainly, in the first half of the 20th century, this may have been deeply satirical, but as newspaper companies flourished under the old advertising-driven business model, a culture developed around the figure of the foreign correspondent as an intrepid, stiff-upper-lipped adventurer reporting back from distant places. As Williams remarks (2011: 93), foreign correspondents themselves often cultivated this image through their memoirs, with colourful stories of dodging bullets and ducking for cover in their lone quest for the truth. Indeed, as Zelizer has observed, journalism is a profession that defines itself through the shared discourse of its practice and collective interpretations of key public events (1993: 219).

News agencies have always been a part of this romance but today, together with a few newspapers such as the *Financial Times* and *New York Times*, they are among the few news outlets to maintain a truly global network of foreign correspondents. The past two decades of social media disruption during which most news organisations struggled to find a new business model and imposed swingeing financial cuts, has spelt the virtual demise of the foreign correspondent in the newspaper and broadcasting world. As the British journalist Colin Freeman lamented, there are today far more people writing about foreign correspondents than there are actually doing it (2016). The figures are stark. In the years after World War II, more than 2,000 US journalists were working in foreign postings, not least as they rushed to Saigon to cover the war in Vietnam. Today, few American newspapers or broadcasters maintain a foreign correspondent outside major centres such as Moscow, London and Beijing, while the same is true for much of the European media. This steady decline in numbers – and a corresponding fall in foreign news – prompted the BBC's former Director of News Richard Sambrook to pose the question (2010): "Are foreign correspondents redundant?" Today, the news agencies represent the last outpost and ensure that they have not entirely died out as a breed. But, as will be examined in the body of this book, their numbers have been diminishing, their role has been changing and the excesses that Evelyn Waugh depicted are well and truly over.

A rich history of scoops

The cliché goes that journalists write the first rough draft of history[4] and that is certainly the case with news agencies. They can all lay claim to an illustrious past full of extraordinary scoops and outstanding journalism. In 1865, the AP was first to tell the world of the assassination of Abraham Lincoln, with its reporter Lawrence Gobright reporting first hand from the blood-stained box at Ford's Theatre. Reuters claims to have been the first to relay the news to European audiences, albeit

12 days later.[5] AP was first with the news of the bombing of Pearl Harbor, the fall of the Shah of Iran and the death of Pope John Paul II (Curley, 2007: 18). Reuters was the first to report the building of the Berlin Wall in 1961 by a margin of eight minutes (Read, 1992: 377), a lifetime in news agency journalism. This was the news flash:

THE EAST-WEST BERLIN BORDER WAS CLOSED EARLY TODAY

And equally, it was the first to break news in 1989 that the Wall was to come down (ibid: 394). Reuters had even beaten by nine minutes the local East German news agency ADN[6] a few days earlier with news that the Communist leader Erich Honecker had resigned. One of AFP's first major scoops came with a news flash on the death of Josef Stalin in 1953 thanks to its monitoring of Radio Moscow's domestic broadcast feed from Paris; and in 1972, AFP trounced all its rivals with news that all the Israeli hostages seized at the Munich Olympics had been killed.

This rich history of major news scoops since the emergence of international news agencies more than 150 years ago, is why generations of journalists have relied on them to be the first to deliver fast, accurate and impartial news. In practical terms, the agencies supply the raw copy for other major news organisations – especially live broadcasters – to feed off as a story is breaking. Yet to the public, these global institutions, with their power to influence the news agenda and frame major stories, remain largely invisible. That in itself is no coincidence. It is in the interest of the news organisations that subscribe to the agencies for the public to assume that they are using their own stories, their own still images or their own video. It can indeed be frustrating for an agency journalist to see his or her story featured in a newspaper with someone else's byline or the infamous phrase "by our foreign staff." It is, however, an implicit part of the business model and a phenomenon that agency journalists quickly come to realise is the norm on routine stories. When it comes to scoops, however, the expectation is that a newspaper or broadcaster is honourable enough to credit the news agency that delivered it. Certainly, in my time, failure to give proper credit could lead to some very terse conversations with other news organisations. The cruel joke was that special correspondents parachuted in by newspapers to cover a conflict would file their report back to head office along the lines "I ducked for cover as the bullets whizzed above my head (pick up agencies) …" By the same token, if a "straight" Reuters news story told in impartial terms was twisted and spun by another news organisation for reasons of propaganda or political gain, stern letters were written.

The same measure of invisibility is also true in the world of academic literature in journalism and media studies. Despite the agencies' core role in relaying the news over the past years, and their continued prominence behind the scenes in today's social media landscape, the main focus of research can be found in historical accounts of their past. This book draws on many of those invaluable works, not least that by the Reuters authorised historian the late Donald Read, whose work *The Power of News*[7] first published in 1992 ends more or less with the fall of the Berlin Wall, well before the 2008 takeover by the Toronto-based Thomson Corporation.[8] Other historical accounts include a volume on the Associated Press featuring chapters on key news events covered by the agency, ranging from the crash of the Hindenburg airship and fall of Saigon to photographer Nick Ut's[9] disturbing image of a napalm attack in Vietnam and Jeff Widener's picture of the Chinese demonstrator facing down a tank in Tiananmen Square[10] (Halberstam, 2007); and the 1992 history of AFP written by two of its most senior editors Jean Huteau and Bernard Ullmann. A second collection of literature is represented by former agency journalists or executives who have sought to tell the "inside story" of life on the editorial coalface. Typical of these is *Breaking News: How the Wheels Came off at Reuters*, written by former journalists Brian Mooney and the late Barry Simpson (2003), a volume the *Financial Times* described as "an incredible story of arrogance, missed opportunities, and the loss of a dominant global market position." The former editor of Bloomberg, Matt Winkler partnered with the ex-banker Michael Bloomberg to write the 1997 autobiography *Bloomberg by Bloomberg*, describing the creation and rapid growth of the agency which would prove to be such a thorn in Reuters side.

Academic examination of the field tends to deal with agencies in the context of the internationalisation and/or globalisation of news (e.g. Bielsa's historical overview, 2008). A similar approach is taken by Kevin Williams in *International Journalism* (2011) which explores international reporting and foreign correspondents. One of the book's chapters, *The Big Three: The Organisational Structure of International Journalism,* focuses specifically on the traditional agencies. Williams tackles the colonial past of agencies such as Reuters and the demise of their news cartel in the 1930s and explores the changes in the first years of the 21st century. Hachten and Scotton also tackle issues of international journalism and globalisation in their 2011 volume *The World News Prism: Challenges of Digital Communication*. By far, the largest body of work is by Oliver Boyd-Barrett, with major books published in 1980, 1998 and 2004. His pursuit of the subject has continued but has also focused on media imperialism. The 1998 volume, *The Globalisation of News* (with Terhi Rantanen), explores through a series of contributed chapters news agencies as agents of globalisation, their role in politics and their role in defining the news agenda. The lead authors update this in a 2004 paper (also available as a chapter in *International News in the 21st Century* edited by Paterson and Sreberny) and then again in 2013 in *Media: An Introduction* edited by Abertazzi and Cobley. As Rantanen observed (2019: 15):

> In the early 21st century, it is very difficult to find current research on news agencies and we very much rely on that which was carried out several decades ago.

This book attempts to go beyond historical accounts to answer some of the more difficult questions facing international news agencies today, to explore business strategies, editorial strategies and actual practice through the eyes of their top editors. What is the agencies' role in today's world of fake news, polarised public discourse and widespread distrust in the media? How have they tackled the disruptions wrought by social media that have undermined the business models of so many established media players (who are also their major clients)? And have they adapted to the new environment or are they an anachronism left over from a bygone age of journalism?

One aspect of news agency life is certainly changing. In that bygone age, it was difficult to avoid the impression that the agencies were a man's world, with the carefully cultivated culture of the macho foreign correspondent and the equally tough stereotype of the male "desker" back at head office handling stories from the field. In the days when copy was phoned in, it was often the case that women manned the switchboard and took dictation from male correspondents in faraway places. Today, there is an increasing emphasis on diversity in the newsroom. Two of the agencies, Reuters and AP, have new editors leading their news operations – Reuters appointed Italian Alessandra Galloni, the first woman Editor-in-Chief in its history, in April 2021, while AP appointed Julie Pace as its Executive Editor and Senior Vice President in September 2021 (the third consecutive woman to lead the AP's worldwide news operation). AFP's global news director between 2014 and 2019, the late Michele Leridon, was the first woman to take the top editorial job at the French agency. Leridon had been a champion of women in the media and was equally focused on tackling the under-representation of women in stories. On her death in 2021, AFP's former CEO Emmanuel Hoog paid tribute to Leridon, saying she was "the standard-bearer for a generation of women who fought to break through the glass ceiling in senior posts." Today, all three agencies publicly commit to diversity in terms of their newsrooms and voice a conviction that it is essential to the actual practice of good journalism. Reuters states in its editorial handbook (2008: 15):

> While politics has no place in our newsrooms, diversity does. We welcome the varying perspectives, insights and considerations that diversity of gender, ethnicity, religion, sexual orientation, upbringing, age, marital or parental status, customs and culture bring to the debate about the news we gather.

Issues of practical journalism aside, there are equally pressing questions about the geo-political role of the news agencies. As the truly global organisations such as Reuters and the Associated Press grew in importance, their extensive communication networks became one of the drivers of globalisation. But their unfettered power behind the scenes has also led to criticism that they have been agents of cultural imperialism, that they have established de facto monopolies or cartels, and that they moved aggressively into domestic markets, squeezing out smaller competition. This is certainly true in terms of video images from faraway places where until recently[11] APTN, the Associated Press's wholesale television news agency, and Reuters Television have for more than two decades enjoyed a virtual duopoly. As Paterson observed (2011: 18):

> The images we all share, and which substantially shape our political, economic and cultural lives, come almost entirely (never completely) from two similar newsrooms in London. That is a process of globalization, and a process of media imperialism. And it is, oddly, all but absent from the last three decades of discussion of globalization.

But despite this hidden power behind the scenes and their glamorous tradition of scoops, not all has been rosy on the bottom line. Most of the agencies have struggled to come to terms with the rapidly changing business and media environment. Profitability has come under pressure as their traditional wholesale customers have been subject to deep cost cutting and consolidation, while ordinary citizens armed with little more than a mobile phone have been able to perform the agencies' core task of reporting from remote corners of the globe. Just as newspapers and broadcasters have cut back hard on the number of foreign correspondents, so too the agencies' traditional clients have often faced the decision whether to maintain the cost of subscribing to two international news agencies (which for many years had been the norm) or reducing this to just one. Galloni and Pace face serious challenges at Reuters and AP as financial constraints continue to impose pressure on editorial costs, with both agencies accused by critics of cutting back foreign news gathering too harshly under the watch of their predecessors.

It is therefore time to take a fresh look at the world's international news agencies and explore inside these omnipresent yet largely invisible organisations that have traditionally preferred to stay out of the limelight.

Chapter overview

What was to become an acrimonious battle for supremacy between Reuters and Bloomberg in the provision of financial news is one I witnessed at first hand, not least at the turn of the century when I worked for Reuters in the United States, a time when Bloomberg was very much in the driving seat. Throughout the writing of this book, I have been conscious of the tensions between my ability to see the agency world from the inside as a former journalist and the discipline of a considered academic analysis. In the chapters that follow, I have done my best to negotiate these tensions in a way that I hope sheds new light on the news agencies without delivering a Reuters-centric view of the world. From a methodological perspective, research has been based on an intensive search and review of existing literature, coupled with analysis of news stories about the agencies and current media trends. This has been complemented by interviews with senior news agency journalists and news executives, both on and off the record.

The first chapter, "From carrier pigeons to social media," sets the historical context for the investigation of the role of news agencies today. It includes their origins, born ironically out of the demand for financial news that, after more than a century dominated by coverage of what might be called "general news," was to throw a financial lifeline to Reuters and spark the emergence of its arch rival Bloomberg. The chapter explores the agencies' colonial past, government interference and their critical role in the formation of the Anglo-American objectivity paradigm. Normative values such as impartiality have come under consistent attack in today's era of social media in which audiences have come to expect a more emotionally driven and opinionated form of news. News agency journalism has for many years represented a "plain vanilla" style of fact-based reporting shorn of adjectives and value judgements. The question is whether this is still valid and whether audiences still want it. Karin Wahl-Jorgensen has suggested that objectivity has frequently been interpreted as excluding certain values through the journalistic narrative and has been widely considered to be (albeit wrongly) the polar opposite of emotion (2020: 176). She suggests, however, that we are today experiencing an "emotional turn" in journalism studies (2020), raising the question whether the traditional form of agency journalism is still a viable policy given the broader news environment (a theme that is explored in detail in Chapters 2 and 3). The first chapter positions the main news agencies at the start of the 21st century, a period in which Reuters was losing its way, Bloomberg was experiencing a meteoric rise to power and AP was starting to feel the pain of cuts in domestic newspaper markets. As such, it sets out the technological, editorial and commercial pressures undermining traditional operations and business models that were to lead to a period of introspection, major strategic review and change.

Chapter 2, "Weathering the storm: Can more than 150 years of tradition save the news agencies?" focuses on how the news agencies are attempting to adapt their business models to the world of social media. It examines their recent financial performance, challenges and opportunities posed by the disruption of the past two decades – the contraction of their traditional wholesale client base in the shape of traditional print publications but also the surprising rise in audience numbers for traditional broadcast news bulletins. For Reuters and Bloomberg periodic crises in the financial sector have also put a strain on earnings, together with uncertainty during the COVID-19 pandemic over whether banks will continue to finance large areas of office space (equipped with agency terminals and news feeds) or will shift towards more of its staff working from home. The chapter analyses the three main strategies that are emerging: the agencies' attempt to embrace the digital age and seek out new markets, to cut costs, and to try to make a virtue of their long tradition in impartial, fact-based news gathering. In celebrating its 175th anniversary, AP noted how it marked almost two centuries of "advancing the power of factual journalism."[12] To what extent do news agencies risk cannibalising their traditional wholesale market by their forays into the retail sector, direct to consumers? Do cuts in editorial staffing undermine the ability to cover the news without leaving the agencies exposed to reputational damage? And is there still a market for impartial, fact-based news in a social media environment in which, emotion, opinion and polarised debate appear to be the new norm?

Chapter 3, "Back to the future: Social media, fact-checking and plain vanilla journalism," shifts the focus from the business of news to editorial practice and focuses on issues of disinformation, manipulation of material and trust, the latter being arguably the most valuable commodity at agencies' disposal. It explores how they handled some of the biggest challenges of the past years, namely the Trump election campaign and COVID-19 pandemic, two long-running stories which have unleashed a veritable tidal wave of disinformation, fake news and conspiracy theories. The chapter goes beyond these examples to shine a spotlight on their emerging policies on fake news, verification and transparency. News agencies have had their fair share of their own scandals around fake news and manipulation of images in the past. But is this a business opportunity in which they can underscore their traditional reputation for accuracy, impartiality and verification? Or have consumers of news lost faith in such values and are they looking for a different, more engaged, more opinionated approach to the news that sits uncomfortably with the notions of objectivity and detachment? The chapter explores the agencies' approach to these issues, how they are handling the torrent of user-generated content that is now flooding into their newsrooms and how they are managing the process of verification. The chapter also examines how the news agencies have adapted their codes of practice to take account of social media, both in terms of how it is incorporated into the mainstream news file but also how correspondents engage with social media platforms such as Twitter and Facebook. As such, the agencies are treading a narrow line between exploiting the advantages of social media and trying to avoid the numerous potential pitfalls.

Chapter 4, "Collaboration, community and state actors," explores how the news gathering environment is changing with the emergence of collaborative news networks, including, for example, those pulled together to sift through the enormous data leaks that made up what became known as the "Panama Papers," "Paradise Papers" and most recently "Pandora Papers," other forms of news alliances and the rise of state actors. In this context, do the international news agencies still have a dominant role in today's news ecology and is their hegemonic Western perspective of news from faraway places (which is deeply rooted in their colonial past) finally being challenged? The chapter examines the emerging new players and alternative approaches to global journalism, including community-based news organisations that have sprung up online. It considers whether the agencies' forays into investigative and long-form journalism are compatible with their core mission of "hard" breaking news. And it explores issues of soft power as government-backed news operations such as China's CGTN embark on ambitious global expansion plans in the face of growing suspicion from Western regulators.

The concluding chapter, "News agencies – rooted in the past and looking to the future," pulls together the strands of analysis and addresses the crucial question of whether news agencies are succeeding in adapting to the social media environment or whether they are now an anachronism, still firmly rooted in a bygone age before the disruption of traditional media. Do they still write the first draft of history and are they still the gatekeepers who control the world's flow of news?

Notes

1. The British architect Sir Edwin Lutyens designed the 1939 Portland Stone building that served as Reuters head office for six decades. Reuters sold the property and moved its headquarters to the London financial district known as Canary Wharf in 2005 although most of editorial had already moved into 200 Gray's Inn Road, also the base of Independent Television News (ITN). It has since moved again within Canary Wharf.
2. In 1981, Michael Bloomberg left Salomon Brothers and founded Innovative Market Systems, a computerised system providing real-time market data and analytics to Wall Street financial firms. He launched his first terminal in 1982 and the news operation in 1990.
3. William Boot set off to cover the war in the fictional African country Ishmaelia with a ton of baggage, a canoe and a "cleft stick" to carry his dispatches. For journalists, it has become a lasting symbol of the lengths they will go to in order to bring back a story from faraway places.
4. The origins of the phrase "first rough draft of history" are not entirely clear but it was popularised by the publisher and co-owner of the *Washington Post* Philip L. Graham during the 1960s. It had also, however, been used repeatedly in the newspaper during the 1940s (Shafer, 2010).
5. AP had a contract with Reuters to supply news from America which was to be sent across the Atlantic by the fastest steamer available.
6. The Allgemeiner Deutscher Nachrichtendienst was the East German state news agency in the German Democratic Republic supplying news to the nation's newspapers and news broadcasters.
7. On the book's publication, Reuters bought 20,000 copies and gave one to each of its clients throughout the world.
8. For ease of reading, when discussing the news, I refer to Reuters during the rest of the book rather than the Thomson Reuters Corporation. Within the company's current corporate structure, Reuters News is one of five "reportable customer segments" which includes an events business.

9. Nik Ut retired after a 51-year career with AP in 2017. He was 21-years-old when he took the picture of the then nine-year-old Kim Phuc running down a road in Vietnam with her body burning after a napalm attack on her village. After taking the picture, Ut rushed her to hospital, where doctors saved her life. The two were reunited in 1989 when Phuc was a medical student in Cuba.
10. Widener tells the story of his "tank man" picture and his coverage of Tiananmen Square on his website. See: http://jeffwidener.com/stories/2016/09/tankman/
11. AFP has attempted in recent years to make substantial inroads into the agency television business, building up a strong presence in video. See Chapter 1, p. 31 and Chapter 2, p. 49.
12. See: https://www.ap.org/press-releases/2021/ap-celebrates-175-years-of-advancing-the-power-of-facts

References

Bartram, J., 2003. News agency wars: The battle between Reuters and Bloomberg. *Journalism Studies*, *4*(3), pp. 387–399.

Bielsa, E., 2008. The pivotal role of news agencies in the context of globalization: A historical approach. *Global Networks*, *8*(3), pp. 347–366.

Bloomberg, M. and Winkler, M., 1997. *Bloomberg by Bloomberg*. New York: J Wiley.

Boyd-Barrett, O., 1980. *The international news agencies* (Vol. 13). London: Constable & Robinson.

Boyd-Barrett, O., Palmer, M. and Rantanen, T., 1998. *The globalization of news*. London: Sage Publications.

Boyd-Barrett, O. and Rantanen, T., 2004. News agencies as news sources: A reevaluation. In Sreberny, A. & Paterson, C. (Eds.), *International news in 21st century* (pp. 31–46). Eastleigh: John Libbey Publishing.

Curley, T., 2007. Preface. In *Breaking news: How the Associated Press has covered war, peace and everything else*. New York: Princeton Architectural Press.

Freeman, C., 2016. Job wanted, will travel. *British Journalism Review*, *27*(3), pp. 43–46.

Hachten, W.A. and Scotton, J.F., 2011. *The world news prism: Challenges of digital communication*. Chichester: John Wiley & Sons.

Halberstam, D., 2007. *Breaking news: How the Associated Press has covered war, peace, and everything else*. New York: Princeton Architectural Press.

Huteau, J. and Ullmann, B., 1992. *AFP: Une histoire de l'Agence France-Presse*. Paris: Robert Laffont.

Mooney, B. and Simpson, B., 2003. *Breaking news: How the wheels came off at Reuters*. Chichester: Capstone Publishing Ltd.

Palmer, M., 2019. *International news agencies: A history*. Cham, Switzerland: Springer International Publishing.

Paterson, C.A., 2011. *The international television news agencies: The world from London*. New York: Peter Lang.

Rantanen, T., 2019. *News agencies from telegraph bureaus to cyberfactories*. Oxford Research Encyclopedia of Communication. Retrieved 28 December 2021, from https://oxfordre.com/communication/view/10.1093/acrefore/9780190228613.001.0001/acrefore-9780190228613-e-843

Read, D., 1992. *The power of news: The history of Reuters*. Oxford: Oxford University Press.

Reuters. 2008. Reuters handbook of journalism. http://handbook.reuters.com/index.php/Main_Page

Sambrook, R., 2010. *Are foreign correspondents redundant? The changing face of international news*. Oxford: Reuters Institute for the Study of Journalism.

Shafer, J., 2010. Who said it first. *Slate*, 30 August 2010. https://slate.com/news-and-politics/2010/08/on-the-trail-of-the-question-who-first-said-or-wrote-that-journalism-is-the-first-rough-draft-of-history.html

Wahl-Jorgensen, K., 2020. An emotional turn in journalism studies? *Digital Journalism*, 8(2), pp. 175–194.

Williams, K., 2011. *International journalism*. London: Sage.

Zelizer, B., 1993. Journalists as interpretive communities. *Critical Studies in Media Communication*, 10(3), pp. 219–237.

1 From carrier pigeons to social media

> The founders of the early telegraph agencies in Europe, Messrs Havas, Reuter and Wolff, were cosmopolitans of their time ... they knew something about publishing, journalism and business: in short, they were the dot.com businessmen of their age.
>
> Terhi Rantanan (2009: 30)

Introduction

It started with a distinctly analogue combination of carrier pigeons and semaphore, a Frenchman named Charles-Louis Havas and his business-savvy realisation that there was money to be made in gathering, distributing and selling news and stock price information to European newspapers. And so, in 1835, Agence Havas was founded as the first international news agency,[1] soon to be joined in 1849 by the Berlin-based Wolffs Telegraphisches Bureau and in 1851 by Reuters. Within just a few years, the three news agencies would expand their reach by embracing the emerging technology of the telegraph and then the first transatlantic undersea cables linking Europe to the United States. Across the Atlantic, the Associated Press came into being in 1846 when five New York City newspapers joined forces to finance a pony express route to deliver news of the war between the United States and Mexico. The race to be first to provide news around the world had begun.

It is a race that has continued for more than 150 years and one that at every turn has seen international news agencies embrace the very latest technology in a bid to outpace the competition. Today news agencies have some of the most advanced communications systems in the world and "beats" are measured in seconds. It is a far cry from the mid-19th century when foreign correspondents such as William Howard Russell were sending dispatches from the Crimean War by

DOI: 10.4324/9781003029656-2

letter, with the result that they could take up to three weeks to arrive back at the editorial headquarters of *The Times* in London via horse and steamer.[2]

These fledgling news agencies, riding the wave of rapidly developing technology and the expansion of daily newspapers, quickly added "hard news" stories to their repertoire of stock market reports and prices and soon became known for speed, accuracy and straight forward reporting. By the time of the Franco-Prussian war (1870–1871), the idea of a foreign correspondent's letter or dispatch was becoming a thing of the past and British newspaper readers expected news from overseas to be available for the next day's edition (Williams, 2011: 53). The offering of news was beginning to take in a now familiar diet of wars and disasters, ranging from floods and earthquakes to street riots and strikes. In 1883, Reuters correspondents were sent a message from its editorial headquarters[3] that might almost have been written today:

> It is requested that the bare facts be first telegraphed with the utmost promptitude, and as soon as possible afterwards a descriptive account, proportionate to the gravity of the incident. Care should, of course, be taken to follow the matter up.
> (cited in Read, 1992: 101)

The first part of this chapter focuses in more detail on the development of the news agencies, how they contributed to the rise of globalisation and their pivotal role in setting the values and practice norms of Anglo-American journalism, norms that had held largely uncontested until the rapid emergence of social media in the 21st century. The second part explores the challenges to those norms that news agencies have had to cope with during the most recent decades, challenges that have been wrought by wide sweeping societal, economic, political and technological changes that almost overnight threw their traditional business model into question.

Birth of the agencies

The emergence and development of international news agencies since the middle of the 19th century bears an uncanny resemblance to preoccupations in today's media landscape. The agencies have at times acted as a cartel, monopolies or duopolies, as has been the case with wholesale television news footage where the market has effectively been dominated by Reuters and AP operations (until a recent challenge by AFP); they have been early adopters of new technology, embracing at first the telegraph and since then every advance in communications to speed up the transmission of stories and images; they have at times been funded, both secretly and openly, by governments and continually been confronted with censorship at times of war; they have been instrumental in establishing a style of "plain vanilla" journalism and spreading Western news values around the world both in colonial and post-colonial times; their adherence to fact-based reporting has been seen as a core strength and yet has often been criticised, especially when it comes to the discipline of presenting opposing sides of a sensitive story, sometimes at times of conflict leading to charges of lack of patriotism; they have been content to operate behind the scenes in day-to-day news gathering but have stood up publicly against harassment, imprisonment and, sadly, the murder of their own correspondents.

It is unlikely that Charles-Louis Havas had an inkling of what was to come when he set up Bureau Havas in 1832, an agency which was to become the precursor of today's Agence France-Presse.[4] While initially the goal at Havas was to translate foreign newspapers for the growing French press, within three years it was producing its own news in the name of L'Agence Havas. Foreshadowing what was to become the agency ethos of speed and accuracy, Havas's watchword was "vite et bien."[5] Soon Paul Julius Reuter, who had been a sub-editor at Havas, and Bernhard Wolff, also a Havas employee, had launched their own rival agencies in London and Berlin, respectively. All three could ride the wave of strong growth in Europe's printed press and growing demand for news which was rapidly becoming a commodity that the likes of Havas, Reuter and Wolff could sell. At the same time, they could exploit the fast developing telegraph network, from where the language of "wire" services and "cables" would stem. Indeed, the first Havas stories appeared in French newspapers in 1853 as "Dépêches télégraphiques privés" (Bielsa, 2008: 351). The first experimental telegraph system had been invented in the 1790s by a French engineer Claude Chappe (a sort of semaphore system), while the first commercial electronic telegraph was established by the mid-1840s by the British scientists Charles Wheatstone and William Cooke (Parry, 2011: 197).[6] But the true advance came with the laying of the first major submarine cable link from Dover to Calais in 1851 and the first reliable transatlantic cable in 1865 (ibid: 200). It was because the telegraph networks expanded so rapidly in Britain, France and Germany that the three fledgling European agencies were able to break out of a national framework and internationalise their operations so quickly (Williams, 2011: 51), starting to "follow the cable" to the United States, then Africa and India in the 1860s and China, South America and

Japan in the 1870s (ibid). Indeed, "follow the cable" would become one of the watchwords of Julius Reuter (Palmer, 2019: 13). During the Mexican-American war of 1846, there were no telegraph networks in the immediate vicinity to rely on. News dispatches originated in Veracruz, crossed the Gulf of Mexico by boat and landed at Mobile, Alabama where they were met by a pony express rider to beat the US mail coach to Richmond and the telegraph terminus. The riders were only paid if they arrived 24 hours ahead of the mail.[7]

Those early years of relaying messages from country to country by homing pigeon or pony express may have become part of the news agency legend and the stuff of film.[8] But the real expansion was driven by the industrialisation of the mid-19th century. As Palmer observes in his history of news agencies (2019: 12):

> Pigeons, boats and ponies nonetheless remained part of a romantic mythology of transmission. Less romantic, telegraph networks were, with the railways (or in US parlance, railroads), the real accelerators of messages, people and goods across time and space.

Establishing news values and norms

The emerging power of the news agencies, combined with the technological limitations of the telegraphic system of communications, had a profound effect in establishing the style of reporting and what were to become deeply entrenched Anglo-American norms of journalism. Those norms have been consistently challenged, especially in the emotion-driven era of social media, and Chapter 3 will explore in detail how the news agencies are addressing this challenge. But the concept of objectivity remains core to discussions about journalism as a profession and works across national frontiers (Maras, 2013: 5). The origins of what has loosely been termed the "objectivity paradigm" are disputed both historically and in the academic field of journalism studies, but it is clear that a series of parallel developments in the United States and Britain contributed to what was to become a reliance on fact-based journalism. This was the age of Darwin, positivism, the primacy of reason over the senses and a growing belief in scientific facts. Schudson (1978) characterises journalists at the turn of the century as "naïve empiricists" who believed in facts as aspects of the world itself, rather than human statements about the world.

But there were also far more prosaic reasons for the emergence of the objectivity paradigm. The news agencies faced entirely practical considerations of reliability and price as they tried to increase their provision of news and sales to expanding newspaper markets. They soon found that telegraph costs were extremely high, leading to a clipped, truncated style that used as few words as possible. Read notes that in the 1860s it cost as much as £1 per word to send a cable from London to India so that early Reuters cable telegrams to and from the world outside Europe were usually kept to bare essentials (1992: 92). At the same time, early telegraph connections were notoriously unreliable – the first transatlantic cable was too thin and failed after less than one month. So, a fact-based news style based on the "Five Ws" (who, what, when, where and why) became the norm, meaning that if the telegraph broke down, the chances were that the most important part of the story, at the top, would arrive in tact. The style of the inverted pyramid story leading with the five Ws became enshrined as an ideal format, and one that is taught in journalism schools to this day.

In the early days of US press expansion in the first half of the 19th century, enabled by the introduction of the rotary press and then steam-powered press, newspapers were expected to present a partisan viewpoint. But as the new technology of mass printing allowed newspaper barons to increase their circulation and, by extension, potential profits, so they pursued politically less partisan coverage to appeal to a wider readership. Once again, this played into the agencies' hands and their factual news accounts. An emphasis on accuracy and telling a story from more than one perspective also emerged as a selling point for the agencies. Paul Julius Reuter, for example, ensured that he had correspondents covering both sides of the 1859 Franco-Austrian war, gaining him credit for objectivity (Read, 1992: 31).

It is remarkable that many of the tenets of modern journalism, some of which are clearly controversial and contested, emerged during this period of the mid-19th century. The style became known as "wire copy" or in German "Telegrafenstil." It concentrated on the five Ws, told a story from multiple perspectives, eschewed sensation, prized freedom from bias and separated fact from comment. During the early 20th century, the fact-based style became even more deeply entrenched within Anglo-American norms as journalism tried to establish itself as a profession distinct from the emerging discipline of public relations. Joseph Pulitzer endowed the School of Journalism at Columbia University in New York in 1904; Walter Lippmann, the journalist and political commentator, vowed to upgrade the professional dignity of journalists and provide training "in which the ideal of objective testimony is cardinal" (cited by Schudson, 2001: 163). The general manager of the Associated Press, Kent Cooper, who joined AP in 1910, actually encouraged his reporters to use livelier prose, added human interest stories and in the 1920s relaxed the agency's ban on bylines. But while Cooper steered the AP into a more modern age of radio and news photos (Halberstam, 2007: 410), he was steadfast in his adherence to fact-based journalism (cited by Schudson, 2001: 162):

> The journalist who deals in facts diligently developed and intelligently presented exalts his profession, and his stories need never be colorless or dull.

Cooper was even more explicit in a 1943 speech on the AP's future, stating (cited in Kreinberg, 2016):

> I have said that true and unbiased news is the highest original moral concept ever developed in America and given the world. This concept, the AP of the future must fight for, as it has through the years.

Competition and the Agency Alliance Treaty

It didn't take long for the success of the first news agencies to generate competition. In another parallel development to today's personality-driven social media, in which sensationalist news poses a challenge to drier fact-based media, rival news agencies that sprung up in the second half of the 19th century sought to provide a livelier style of news. In the United Kingdom, the Central News Agency, founded in 1863, and Exchange Telegraph (1872) were soon providing competing news services, while Dalziel's news style (set up in 1890) was perceived as being less institutional than that of Reuters and inundated European newspapers with American human interest and sports stories (Palmer, 2019: 59).

The Dalziel threat lasted only three years but the three original European agencies, Reuters, Havas and Wolff had already entered into a series of agreements, the first dating from 1859. Then in 1870, they signed what was became known as the Agency Alliance Treaty, or "ring combination" (Read, 1992: 53). This alliance, which the parties agreed to keep secret, essentially carved up the world in imperial style into spheres of influence. Reuters reigned supreme in the British Empire and Far East, Havas held sway in the French and Portuguese empires, while Wolff's sphere centred on Austria, Scandinavia and Russia. As Williams notes, the alliance allowed the free exchange of news between the three agencies and provided each with a virtual monopoly on news in their territories (2011: 55). One impact of the alliance was initially to marginalise American agencies, specifically the Associated Press (although it was integrated into US news gathering in 1893) and United Press,[9] which was formed in 1907.

It was a cartel that held until the 1930s, through many strains, disputes and financial crises. By the time of its demise, it had been fundamental in setting up a developing global communications infrastructure, spreading a Western-style of journalism and, as part of that, a Western view of the world that reflected that of the colonial powers. Every time the cartel formed an alliance with a smaller national agency to supply news, the members spread and inculcated their news style and values. Boyd-Barrett argues that the unequal news exchange relationships imposed by the dominant Anglo-Franco-American international news agencies on national agencies throughout much of the 19th and 20th centuries was a prime example of "media imperialism" (2014: 1).[10] The agencies were also an important force in consolidating and propagating images of national identity, especially important before the arrival of radio and television. The international information order that grew out of the 60-year-long agency alliance was monopolised by the interests of European traders, businessmen and colonial administrators and the nature of the news reflected this bias (Williams, 2011: 56).

Breaking free of government shackles

By the 1930s, it was clear that the cartel had run its course. One of the driving forces for its demise came from America, where the increasingly powerful AP (although part of the cartel) and United Press expressed their frustration at the dominance of Reuters, its British-centric view of the world and cliché laden stories from the United States about film stars and gangsters. In 1930, AP's general manager Kent Cooper argued for a free market and an end to the "ring"; he was determined to sell news into the Far East and make the organisation a truly global agency (Read, 1992: 172). Despite the tensions, a new agreement was signed in 1932 between Reuters, AP, Havas and Wolff. Within two years, it was already crumbling although the last vestiges survived until 1939.

Cooper's criticism of Reuters went deeper than his resentment of its news file and view of America. In his 1942 account of the Associated Press, *Barriers Down*, he railed against the monopoly of government influenced agencies which were obstructing the free flow of international news and highlighted the immense global influence of the cartel. At its height, Cooper wrote, it was the most powerful international monopoly of the 19th century, setting the agenda and framing the news (1942: 7):

> When Reuter, Havas and Wolff pooled their resources, established complete news agency control of international news, and allotted to themselves the news agency exploitation in all the countries of the world, they brought under their control the power to decide what the people of each nation would be allowed to know of the peoples of other nations and in what shade of meaning the news was to be presented.

A contributing factor to the decline of the cartel was the growing concern about the lack of independence of the European agencies, particularly focusing on Reuters connections to the British government. In the late 1930s, the agency's then head Roderick Jones appealed to the Prime Minister Neville Chamberlain for financial support in the face of European competition (Havas, e.g., was subsidised by the French government) and secured both additional government "subscriptions" and, in 1939, a secret agreement to receive £64,000 from the British Ministry of Information for "propaganda purposes" (Palmer, 2019: 117).

World War II turned out to be a pivotal moment and underscored the government connections. Havas was nationalised when German forces invaded France in 1940 and it became the Office Français d'Information (OFI). Wolff, which had been under government control during World War I, was closed with Hitler's rise to power in 1933 and was essentially replaced by the Nazi-controlled Deutsches Nachrichtenbüro, a propaganda machine for the Third Reich. From 1942, it also effectively controlled OFI. At Reuters, coverage of the war was subject to censorship and Read recounts instances in which the agency suppressed news that might have been against the national interest (1992: 217). The agency was routinely referred to by the Nazi regime as a British propaganda outlet although it actually established a notable reputation for excellent coverage of the war and registered several beats including that of Gestapo chief Heinrich Himmler's offer to surrender to the Western allies on April 28, 1945.

The real victors in the news agency war turned out to be the Associated Press and United Press, reflecting America's growing power on the world stage and benefiting from a US newspaper appetite for news in Europe. The two agencies developed their global networks of correspondents to report on the war, with AP building up its pictures service to produce images of the conflict and United Press focusing on human interest stories (Williams, 2011: 71). They managed to undercut Reuters on price, increasing the already severe financial strains on the British agency (Palmer, 2019: 135). It can be argued that at this time, the Anglo-Franco-German domination of the news agenda had simply been swapped for a US-led hegemony.

The post-war period also saw the two major European agencies, Reuters and Agence France-Presse, seek to shake off their reputation for state control and to establish their true independence. AFP had emerged out of the ashes of Havas and journalists belonging to the French resistance movement had sent its first 220-word dispatch on August 20, 1944 as Allied forces retook Paris (Huteau & Ullmann, 1992: 11). But AFP was state controlled and it took until 1957 for the French parliament to pass a law recognising its independence (and by extension, improving its credibility as a news agency). The statute declared that the agency must not fall under any political, ideological or economic group (Palmer, 2019: 154) and reflected in part an earlier development at Reuters. The British agency had in 1941 agreed so-called Trust Principles with its owners of the time, the Newspaper Proprietors Association and the Press Association.

Those Trust Principles are still in force today and are key to the agency's fierce culture of independence. In 1941, this drive for independence meant escaping the clutches of the British government. Later, after the 1984 flotation of shares on the stock market, it would mean ensuring that foreign powers did not build up a significant stake.[11] The Trust Principles today are little changed from those agreed in 1941 and impose obligations on Reuters and its employees to act at all times with integrity, independence and freedom from bias (Thomson Reuters, 2021). They read as follows:

1 That Reuters shall at no time pass into the hands of any one interest, group or faction;
2 That the integrity, independence and freedom from bias of Thomson Reuters shall at all times be fully preserved;
3 That Reuters shall supply unbiased and reliable news services to newspapers, news agencies, broadcasters and other media subscribers and to businesses, governments, institutions, individuals, and others with whom Reuters has or may have contracts;
4 That Thomson Reuters shall pay due regard to the many interests which it serves in addition to those of the media; and

5 That no effort shall be spared to expand, develop, and adapt the news and other services and products of Thomson Reuters so as to maintain its leading position in the international news and information business.

The final point was put to the test in 2008 when Reuters was taken over by the Canadian Thomson Corporation to form the current Thomson Reuters Corporation. The Reuters Founders Share Company was called into action and controversially agreed to support Thomson's acquisition, concluding that the merger would help secure the financial health of the Reuters business. The then chairman of the Founders Share Company, Pehr Gyllenhammar,[12] said: "The future of Reuters takes precedence over the principles. If Reuters were not strong enough to continue on its own, the principles would have no meaning."

In the post-war years, it was debatable whether Reuters had really shaken off the influence of the British government. A watershed moment came with the 1956 Suez crisis when Egyptian President Gamal Abdel Nasser nationalised the Suez Canal, prompting an invasion by Israel, France and the United Kingdom. Christopher Chancellor,[13] who led Reuters as general manager from 1944 until 1959, issued a note to his journalists after the invasion saying: "Reuters does not represent the British government" (cited in Read, 1992: 270). The historian Read questions whether this statement reflected the fact that opinion over the invasion in Britain was divided or a true commitment to independence. However, there are arguments for the latter interpretation. It was at this time that Reuters stopped referring to British forces as "our troops" (i.e. using instead the neutral formulation "British troops") and in subsequent years Chancellor was keen to emphasise the international nature of Reuters and its independence from the British government. He stated (ibid: 269):

> Reuters is not just a British news service; it is not an organ for presenting British news ... it is an organisation to supply newspapers and radio stations of every country of the world with a truthful and complete service of world news.

AFP went through a similar test with its coverage of Algeria's fight for independence and the Algerian war of 1954–1962. Initially, AFP called Algerian nationalists "outlaws" or "rebels." Such language confirmed perceptions that AFP was still a quasi-official agency (Palmer, 2019: 155). But as the conflict progressed, so AFP's reporting became more even handed although the French government continued to fund the agency indirectly by subscribing to its news services and even in 1960 this still totalled 57% of revenue (ibid: 157).

Translating independence into a style and ethos

The foundations of the agencies' fact-based style of journalism had been laid in the 19th century as they became drivers of the Anglo-American objectivity paradigm. But as the Suez crisis and war in Algeria demonstrated, the use of language can easily reveal biases and undermine any claim to impartiality. What emerged was a series of "style books" in which editors sought to set out guidelines for their respective agency journalists. AP's version was first published in a publicly available version in 1953 although in-house versions can be traced back to 1909. At Reuters, the late Ian Macdowall, chief news editor, compiled a style book that was first published in 1992. In it, he concisely sums up the agency ethos, writing (1992: vii):

> The cardinal principle which should underlie the work of any news agency is honesty. Its file should be accurate as to fact and balanced as to the selection of facts and of background and interpretation used in putting these facts in context.

One key section of the guide, labelled "emotive words," states that some words have emotional significance and should be used with special care in the interest of objectivity (ibid: 55). As an example, Macdowall cited *terrorist, terrorism, extremist* and *extremism*. One man's terrorist, he wrote, is another man's freedom-fighter. Contentious labels, he advised, should be avoided as far as possible. When it came less than a decade later to the September 11 attacks on the United States, I advised as global head of news that we should report the facts and not label the attackers as terrorists. My internal memo to Reuters newsrooms was leaked to the *Washington Post* and a storm engulfed the agency (and me). It was, of course, a hugely insensitive memo, but it reflected a deep-seated agency culture to avoid judging people's motives in stories and rather to describe actions. It would not be the first or last time that Reuters, and other agencies, have become embroiled in controversy over such decisions or use of the word "terrorist."[14] And the value neutral stance has, of course, been routinely questioned in times of conflict. In fact, an analysis of Reuters archive material by Goodman and Boudana, focusing on the agency's coverage of the Arab-Israeli conflict between 1967 and 1982, concluded that the goal of objectivity was less of an absolute principle but rather the subject of internal debates and tensions, often provoked by subscribers' reactions to specific stories (2016: 1).

The agencies' solution to the conundrum of emotive words has been to "outsource" such language to those quoted in a story. Wahl-Jorgensen has referred to this as a "strategic ritual of emotionality," a tacit yet institutionalised and systematic practice by which journalists infuse reporting with emotion (2013: 1). By quoting others, journalists can use such difficult terms and at the same time inject emotion into a story which would otherwise be dry and boring. As the highly respected Macdowall wrote of contentious labels in 1992 (55):

> You can, of course, use such words without inhibition when directly quoting sources that are named or individually identified.

UNESCO and the charge of imperialism

If the news agencies had been agents of imperialism since their founding in the mid-19th century, the charge came out into open public debate in the 1960s and 1970s. This came to a head with the publication in 1980 by UNESCO, the United Nations Educational, Scientific and Cultural Organisation, of the MacBride Report into the global flow of information. In it, Sean MacBride, a Nobel Peace Prize winner and former Irish Foreign Minister, called for a New World Information and Communication Order. Although the section on news agencies was relatively short, the report specifically criticised them for perpetuating an imbalanced picture of global news at the expense of the global South (sometimes referred disparagingly today to as "the West to the rest"). The debate had become increasingly acrimonious and highly politicised, the latter fostered by the growing strength of the Non-Aligned Movement and consolidated around UNESCO's headquarters in Paris (Boyd-Barrett, 1981: 247). Aside from the underlying reproach of a neo-colonial attitude to news, the MacBride Report levelled two main charges. Firstly, that the flow of news was disproportionately dedicated to events in Western nations and that there was very little coverage of events in Africa, Latin America and Asia; and secondly, what coverage there was tended to focus negatively on events including famines, coups and earthquakes. MacBride stated that the news agencies' "massive worldwide operations give them a near monopoly in the international dissemination of news; thus, the world receives some 80% of its news through London, Paris and New York" (1980: 145). In short, the report charged that large areas of the world were being underreported and misrepresented. This had been already observed in the academic world through Galtung and Ruge's pioneering 1965 study on news values which highlighted areas of negativity and conflict, while Elliott and Golding (1974) had identified how Western media focused in developing world news coverage on five main themes: repetitive political and military crises, Western interests, superpower relations, an oversimplified narrative and reference to previous stories (i.e. how breaking news of a coup might echo power struggles of the past).

The news agencies reacted in a typically defensive fashion though some also went on the attack. In their history of AFP, Jean Huteau and Bernard Ullmann said that it had been hard to see how the MacBride report criticisms could be justified. Many AFP correspondents had seen work in Africa as a key point in the development of their career and many had spent their entire time in Africa or Asia (1992: 404). Henri Pigeat, the head of AFP from 1979 to 1986, took a moderate approach but made it clear to UNESCO that any rebalancing of the flow of information from North to South could not be at the expense of, or brought about by limitations to, Western media and Western news agencies (ibid: 405). But at Reuters, Gerald Long, who became Managing Director in 1973, saw the UNESCO push for a new world information order as a threat and pulled no punches. He suggested that the clamour for change was coming from authoritarian countries that censored their own domestic news output, saying "you cannot have repression at home and enlightenment abroad" (cited in Read, 1992: 326).

The UNESCO debate faded in due course and a series of alliances and attempts to bring national news agencies into regional groupings had only moderate success. One grouping was of pan-African agencies (PANA), another the Caribbean News Agency (CANA). But while such alliances and regional exchange agreements did produce more coverage of development stories, the contribution to the flow of news was in the final analysis limited (Williams, 2011: 11). It was only the founding of major new players into the international media market, such as Al-Jazeera in 1996, that would bring a different perspective to the Western-centric view of the world.

Corporate change and the building blocks of today's agency landscape

The UNESCO debate aside, the last two decades of the 20th century were key in determining the modern shape of the main Western agencies. It was a time when the US agencies AP and UPI were briefly in the ascendancy before US newspapers began to run into financial difficulties; a time when AFP was reliant on French government subsidies and when Reuters was struggling financially. It was also a time in which the market for news was becoming increasingly commercialised and deregulated. As part of that climate, the dominance enjoyed by the mainstream news agencies was slowly but surely undermined by the likes of CNN and Al-Jazeera which exploited satellite technology to deliver international news footage to other broadcasters.[15] As a result, the traditional news agencies sought to diversify and expand their operations across an increasingly wide array of news "products," from video and still images to financial news. In seeking to provide the international finance markets with news, agencies such as Reuters and AFP rode the wave of globalisation and were going back to their roots in the first half of the 19th century.

Reuters decision to float its shares on the stock market in 1984 typified this commercialisation of news. Spurred on by the financial information company Telerate, which had raised capital with a public flotation in 1983, the owners of Reuters (a trust in the hands of British, Irish, Australian and New Zealand newspaper groups) were eager to cash in on a hidden treasure "they had discovered in the loft" (Greenslade, 2003: 376). But the public offering was extremely controversial, not least because of the perceived threat to the agency's independence – testimony to the fact that by the 1980s Reuters had thrown off its reputation for being an arm of the British government. The controversy was such that questions were asked in parliament. Austin Mitchell, a Labour Party member of parliament, voiced his concern in a House of Commons debate on January 27, 1984, saying (Hansard, 1984):

> We have the spectacle of greedy men – the press barons – clutching for the glittering cash prizes in this raffle. They are acting irresponsibly and in defiance of solemn commitments that their predecessors gave. In defying those solemn principles, they are plotting to get around the technical and legal obstacles. In so doing they are defying a principle on which Reuters was founded and the ethics and morality with which it has been run for decades.
>
> News is a precious commodity that must be handled with integrity by an independent agency. It should not be distorted, coloured, or subject to the commercial pressures that are likely to result from the flotation.

In the final analysis, a two-tier system was devised to protect the trust principles, the share offering was 2.7 times oversubscribed and

Reuters raised £53 million through the sale of new shares to expand its operations and make acquisitions. The newspaper owners reaped a windfall they could hardly have dreamt of a few years earlier, a windfall that helped them move many of their operations out of the traditional newspaper centre of Fleet Street to new green field sites. News International, owned by Rupert Murdoch, was able to draw on the proceeds of the Reuters flotation to help finance a new plant in East London at Wapping and his drive to defeat the traditional print unions. The move was to provoke one of the most bitter labour disputes of the 1980s.

The competition for dominance

The last years of the 20th century were to be dominated by a wave of expansion, diversification and fierce competition in the media industry. From the perspective of the international news agencies, the drive was to capture the highly profitable market for financial news and be the major provider of still images and video.

i) Serving mammon[16]

The 1980s saw a scramble by the agencies to provide news to the booming financial markets and the world's banking sector as global trade and securities trading took off following the 1971 Smithsonian agreement and free floating of currencies. For a time, the provision of financial news even eclipsed the traditional "general news" reporting and caused rifts and resentment within editorials as investment flowed into "econ" news areas.

Each of the main agencies undertook large-scale investment, both in terms of technology and the acquisition of technology companies. In Reuters case, this was fuelled by the stock flotation and the number of bureaux worldwide at all the agencies expanded rapidly. AP and AFP bolted on financial news through arrangements with specialist financial information organisations, creating AP-Dow Jones (known as AP-DJ) and AFX News.[17] To add to this fiercely competitive mix, where "beats" on routine financial news (e.g. central bank interest rate changes, corporate earnings and economic policy pronouncements) were measured in seconds, a new agency emerged on the scene. Bloomberg Business News, as it was initially called,[18] was founded in 1990 by the former investment banker Michael Bloomberg. As an ex-trader, Bloomberg instinctively understood the needs of the market and the upstart agency quickly became a thorn in the side of

Reuters. Within a few years, the Bloomberg terminal with its combination of yield calculations and financial news became indispensable and was seen as superior to the Reuters version.[19] "The Bloomberg," as it was called, emerged as a highly coveted status symbol for successful traders. AP-DJ, Reuters and Bloomberg soon realised that financial customers were measuring their performance in seconds. At Reuters, journalists would each day receive a list of what were called "competitive timings," cataloguing all the key news stories of the previous day and giving the time of each news alert versus "the opposition." To be five seconds behind on a major interest rate decision by the US Federal Reserve or German Bundesbank was very bad news for the journalists involved. Setting aside the speed of actual reporting, investment was poured into ensuring that the news alerts hit traders' screens without any technical delay across the world the second they were filed. As a journalist covering such news stories in the 1980s and 1990s, these were heady days, beats were celebrated and losses signalled the need to write a note of explanation. Reuters terminals in those days included a series of private pages accessible only to its journalists and the "quality log" statistics were called up with anticipation (and sometimes a sense of dread) each day.[20] Fully aware that political news often moved markets, Bloomberg set up operations in, for example, Washington D.C., thus competing with Reuters and AP on general news as well. The key question, posed by a former European Financial Editor at Reuters, John Bartram,[21] was (2003: 387):

> How did Britain's Reuters, a company with a 150-year history that was once the leader of the financial news agency world, allow an American upstart like Bloomberg, not even 20 years old by the end of the 20th century, to steal up behind it and take the leading, more aggressive role as the 21st century began?

Under its editor Matthew Winkler, Bloomberg revolutionised the agency business and not just by introducing fierce competition to Reuters and AP-DJ. Bloomberg reporters posted their e-mail address and telephone number at the bottom of a story so the reader could follow up with queries. The move was to herald the end of the anonymous agency report and foreshadow today's social media environment in which journalists are expected to maintain a social media presence and be contactable across multiple platforms. Bloomberg also took a leaf out of AP's book and introduced human interest and sports stories, plus weather updates. The terminal built in a messaging system that became highly popular, years before WhatsApp. Traders could even book travel and send flowers over their "Bloomberg" – it became established in their minds as an indispensable tool (Bartram, 2003: 391). In the final analysis, however, it was Bloomberg and Reuters who survived, with Telerate, AP-DJ and AFX, the ultimate casualties, leaving what is still today a virtual duopoly in the provision of global financial news.

ii) The duopoly in video footage, AFP tries to make inroads

By the turn of the century, the wholesale market for news video had also become a clear duopoly, this time with AP and Reuters sharing the spoils (in the guise of AP Television News, headquartered in north London, and Reuters Television). Today, the vast majority of footage included in television news bulletins around the world is likely to have originated in a feed from one of the two agencies, although AFP, a late entrant into the market, has been investing heavily to build up its television output through AFPTV. And in truth, as Paterson observes in his study of television news agencies, a quite significant part of what the audience sees is barely modified at all from the output of the news agencies (2011: 2). They are an essential tool for broadcasters, Paterson argues, omnipresent but substantially invisible (ibid: 10).

The duopoly had arisen from a consolidation and shifts in ownership during the 1990s that saw Reuters buy out Visnews in 1992 and APTN take over Worldwide Television News in 1997. By then, the cinema newsreels, so popular in the 1930s and 1940s, were a thing of the past and broadcasters worldwide were seeking footage for their news bulletins without incurring the expense of foreign bureaux or their own news gathering teams. The agencies such as Visnews had pioneered the use of satellite technology and often provided uplink facilities to other broadcasters from the scene of major breaking news stories. Stephen Claypole, Visnews Editor, said the Tiananmen Square story in 1989 was a watershed moment when the provision of uplink time became a vital business for the agency (cited in Paterson, 2011: 55). But the period was tumultuous, marked by layoffs at Visnews as Reuters increased its control over the agency, and at a fledgling financial television news channel that Reuters eventually wound up in 2002. Reuters Financial TV (known as RFTV) had been launched in 1994 and was aimed at trading rooms. But it was hampered by the need to install satellite dishes at banks to receive the signal and a dwindling number of subscribers. Ironically, it may have survived in today's world of streaming video content. But at the time, Reuters never made the investment required to turn the service into a 24-hour broadcast rival to the dominant CNBC business network, leaving many Reuters journalists with a bitter feeling (Bartram, 2003: 8). By the time of its closure, Reuters Financial Television had become the most expensive and perhaps least watched television service in history (Mooney & Simpson, 2003). By contrast, Bloomberg succeeded in launching a financial television network, ensuring the agency's brand was prominently displayed on screens throughout the banking world.

During the boom years of the 1980s and 1990s, the Reuters and AP wholesale television feeds, together with the accompanying scripts, led to a truly global flow of information that today, despite the advent of social media, still finds its way through broadcast news bulletins into homes worldwide. And as Paterson has observed, it is a phenomenon that has been largely overlooked in the discussion of globalisation (2011: 18):

> The images we all share, and which substantially shape our political, economic and cultural lives, come almost entirely (never completely) from two similar newsrooms in London. That is a process of globalisation, and a process of media imperialism. And it is, oddly, all but absent from the last three decades of discussion of globalisation.

As will be explored later, the image-driven nature of today's media means the news agencies are keen to exploit the business potential of digital video which is taking on an increasingly important role within editorial operations. AP's new executive editor Julie Pace joined the agency in 2007 as a video producer and multimedia political journalist after starting her journalism career at a television network in South Africa. A still open question is to what extent AFP can break the de facto Reuters/APTN duopoly at a time when commercial broadcasters, strapped for cash, are unlikely to subscribe to more than one provider of wholesale video news. The French agency has been investing in video and particularly trying to bridge a gap in US coverage. AFP's Chairman and CEO Fabrice Fries stated in its 2020 annual report (Agence France-Presse, 2020):

> If in 2019 we could say that our video production had reached the same level as that of our two big competitors, in 2020 we can tell clients that they can do perfectly well with just AFP as an agency since this last weakness in geographical coverage is now a thing of the past. That is a considerable change.

iii) News pictures

The renewed foray into financial news and the exponential growth of television services stemmed from the economic boom and technological revolution at the end of the 20th century. News pictures, on the other hand, had a far longer pedigree and became a major business with the ability to transmit images by wire. AP began sending photographs over telephone lines[22] in 1935 in a move driven by its General Manager Kent Cooper (Halberstam, 2007: 411). The first transmission via AP's "Wirephoto" operation in 1935 went to 47 newspapers in 25 states and, as Hal Buell, the head of pictures at AP for 15 years remarked, the service quickly became viewed as indispensable (Buell, 2007: 315). AFP's photo service was created in 1944 by freelance photographers Georges Mélamed, André Raimbaud and Robert Palat, who covered the Liberation of Paris from German occupation.[23] Reuters was the last to develop a pictures service, buying UPI's operation in 1985 after years of complaints by Reuters managers about the lack of images to accompany textual news reports (Read, 1992: 340). Over time, the power of these three mainstream news agencies and their pictures operations helped to dethrone the classic "photos only" agencies Magnum, Sygma and Gamma (Palmer, 2019: 234).

AP photographers captured some of the lasting images of World War II, such as Joe Rosenthal's shot of US marines hoisting the American flag at the Battle of Iwo Jima. As Buell, observed, it became the lasting image of the Pacific War and the three flag raisers who survived the battle were summoned home and hailed as heroes (Buell, 2007: 311). But as so often with "iconic" photos, there was also controversy and the charge that this was a posed picture haunted the image and plagued Rosenthal (ibid). Later AP pictures from Vietnam, with a team led by the legendary Pulitzer Prize winner Horst Faas, put the war onto the front page of every US newspaper. Nik Ut's 1972 photograph of the nine-year-old Vietnamese girl Kim Phuc fleeing a napalm attack became another iconic image of the war. Today, of course, film no longer needs to be developed and images are transmitted almost instantaneously via digital technology uploaded from the scene of the news. Mobile phone pictures from citizens witnessing news stories sometimes capture images before professional photographers can arrive on the scene and "user-generated content" is ubiquitous. As will be examined in the subsequent chapters, the undermining of the agency's business model in, for example, news pictures led to a widespread re-evaluation of the operations that have generated so many enduring images. Costs have been cut relentlessly but AFP and Getty Images in 2021 renewed their long-standing content partnership initiated in 2003. And despite financial pressures, AP, Getty/AFP and Reuters have consistently been rewarded with the prestige of Pulitzer prizes for their news photography.

Conclusion: How the wheels came off

In 2003, two former Reuters journalists, Brian Mooney and the late Barry Simpson, wrote a scathing inside story about how, at the turn of the century, the news agency had lost its way. It was called *Breaking News: How the Wheels Came off at Reuters* and pulled no punches:

> As the Internet age arrived, Reuters found itself without any clear strategy, uncertain whether it was a technology or information company or a bit of both, and unable to exploit its obvious advantages. And while senior managers indulged in high living, major divisions of the company were torn apart by a destructive succession battle.

There was indeed a sense of crisis at Reuters, losing market share rapidly at the hands of Bloomberg, and riven by in-fighting. As the *Financial Times* put it, this was an incredible story of arrogance, missed opportunities, and the loss of a dominant global market position. *Breaking News* was a book that foreshadowed the financial crisis at Reuters that led to its takeover by the Canadian Thomson organisation in 2008.

But while Bloomberg was clearly in the ascendancy, problems were mounting across the board. While the wheels were undoubtedly coming off at Reuters, the same could be said to a more modest extent of its major competitors. The next chapter focuses on the business strategies of the main agencies and explores how they have been coping with the downturn in traditional media markets, periodic crises in the financial markets and a global economic downturn caused by the COVID-19 pandemic. How have they tackled the prevalence of social media and the polarisation of discourse that it embodies? What strategies have they employed to protect their businesses in the face of declining revenues and what new opportunities might have opened up during the months of lockdown as news consumption habits shift?

Some of the answers lie in the more than 170-year history charted in this chapter and the constant threads that run through it – the core values of being independent, delivering fact-based journalism and allowing clients to make their own decisions on the basis of the impartial information presented. Far from being dead, the agencies are putting their money on there being a growing appetite for that type of "plain vanilla" news.

Notes

1. Charles-Louis Havas first created Bureau Havas in 1832, translating foreign news stories for the French press, and developed it into Agence Havas in 1835. Its full title was: Agence des Feuilles Politiques - Correspondance Générale.
2. William Howard Russell, known as one of the first "war correspondents," was an Irish reporter with *The Times*. He spent almost two years covering the Crimean War, including the "Charge of the Light Brigade" at the Battle of Balaclava in 1854. His reporting from the battlefield and conditions endured by British forces caused shock when they arrived in London.
3. In his history of Reuters, Donald Read suggests the instruction may have been written by Baron Herbert de Reuter who took over from his father Paul Julius Reuter, the founder of Reuters. (1992: 100).
4. The first news report under the name Agencé France-Presse was sent in 1944. But by tracing its roots back to Havas AFP can lay claim to being the oldest news agency.
5. Literally "quick and well," and not dissimilar to the modern "fast and accurate."
6. They patented their system in 1837. A new business called the Electric Telegraph Company was set up in 1845 that bought out the patent. Soon dozens of competing companies started to trade in Britain (Parry, 2011: 197).
7. See AP website celebrating its 175th anniversary: https://apimagesblog.com/historical/2021/1/30/ap-at-175-a-photographic-history
8. In a 1940 film entitled *A Dispatch from Reuters*, Paul Julius Reuter, played by Edward G Robinson, is depicted using homing pigeons to plug a gap in the telegraph network between Aachen and Brussels.
9. United Press was founded in 1907 and became United Press International or UPI in 1958 when it absorbed its rival International News Service, founded in 1909 by newspaper publisher William Randolph Hearst. At one stage in the 1960s it had 2,000 employees and was a mainstream competitor to Reuters, AP and AFP. But it was subject to a series of cuts, bankruptcies and takeovers in the last two decades of the 20th century.
10. Boyd-Barrett argues that the term "media imperialism" should not be thought of as a single theory but rather as a field of study that incorporates different theories about media and empire (2014: 14).
11. When Reuters became a publicly traded company on the London Stock Exchange and Nasdaq in 1984, a new structure was put in place to uphold independence. A new company was formed and named "Reuters Founders Share Company Limited," its purpose being to hold a "Founders Share" in Reuters.

12. Between 1970 and 1994, Pehr Gyllenhammar was CEO and chair of the Swedish company Volvo.
13. Chancellor died in 1989. *The Times* obituary said: "Chancellor gave Reuters a position as a world news agency which Britain's diminished role after the end of the Second World War did not make it easy to sustain."
14. Exactly 20 years after the September 11 attacks, fresh controversy arose when two Thomson Reuters executives signed a covenant expressing the company's support for the British armed forces. Journalists at Reuters reacted with a mixture of uproar, disbelief and dismay, arguing it threatened the Trust Principles. Within two weeks, the move had been rescinded.
15. Cable News Network (CNN) was launched in Atlanta in 1980; Al-Jazeera, based in Doha, Qatar, followed in 1996.
16. In their 1998 book, *The Globalisation of News*, Boyd-Barrett, Palmer and Rantanen described Reuters as lying midway between Mammon and Mercury.
17. AP linked up with Dow Jones to increase its coverage of financial news in 1967. The AP-DJ agreement came to an end in 2008. AFP entered into a similar arrangement with the British domestic agency Extel in 1991. It was sold to Thomson Financial in 2006.
18. The agency was renamed Bloomberg News in 1997.
19. Reuters had introduced its "monitor" with foreign exchange and money market rates back in 1973 and added news a year later. In 1981, it introduced a dealing system for currencies which effectively ended what had been a telephone market for foreign exchange.
20. In the late 1990s, Reuters was accused of obtaining Bloomberg data improperly through its operation called Reuters Analytics in Stamford, Connecticut. A New York court concluded after a lengthy FBI investigation that no charges should be brought. But the experience left Reuters deeply shocked and raised internal questions about management control (Mooney & Simpson, 2003).
21. From 1989 to 1995, Bartram worked in Reuters London "Quality Unit" monitoring and writing assessments of its economic and financial news and comparing it with opposition news agencies, including Bloomberg.
22. The AP's original photo service set up in 1927 delivered pictures by mail and by hand.
23. AFP first used a machine called the Belinograph to transmit pictures by telephone and radio links.

References

Agence France-Presse. 2020. Annual report. https://view.afp.com/2020-annual-report/home-page/p/1

Bartram, J., 2003. News agency wars: The battle between Reuters and Bloomberg. *Journalism Studies*, *4*(3), pp. 387–399.

Bielsa, E., 2008. The pivotal role of news agencies in the context of globalization: A historical approach. *Global Networks*, *8*(3), pp. 347–366.

Boyd-Barrett, O., 1981. Western news agencies and the "media imperialism" debate: What kind of data-base? *Journal of International Affairs*, 35(2), pp. 247–260.

Boyd-Barrett, O., 2014. *Media imperialism*. London: Sage.

Buell, H., 2007. Why not a camera? In Halberstam, D. (Ed.), *Breaking News: How the Associated Press Has Covered War, Peace, and Everything Else*. New York: Princeton Architectural Press.

Cooper, K., 1942. *Barriers down*. New York: Farrar & Rinehart Incorporated.

Elliott, P. and Golding, P., 1974. Mass communication and social change: The imagery of development and the development of imagery. In De Kadt, E. and Williams, G. (Eds.), *Sociology and Development* (pp. 229–254). London: Routledge.

Galtung, J. and Ruge, M.H., 1965. The structure of foreign news: The presentation of the congo, Cuba and Cyprus crises in four Norwegian newspapers. *Journal of Peace Research*, 2(1), pp. 64–90.

Goodman, G. and Boudana, S., 2016. The language of objectivity: Reuters internal editorial discussions on terminology in the Arab–Israeli conflict. *Journalism*, 1, p. 17.

Greenslade, R., 2003. *Press gang: How newspapers make profits from propaganda*. London: Macmillan.

Halberstam, D., 2007. *Breaking news: How the Associated Press has covered war, peace, and everything else*. New York: Princeton Architectural Press.

Hansard. 1984. Reuters flotation. https://hansard.parliament.uk/Commons/1984-01-27/debates/a4273968-d281-44a8-b9e8-186f21b9b46f/Reuters(Flotation)

Huteau, J. and Ullmann, B., 1992. *AFP: Une histoire de l'Agence France-presse*. Paris: Robert Laffont.

Kreinberg, J., 2016. A history of media innovation and press freedom. https://insights.ap.org/whats-new/a-history-of-media-innovation-and-press-freedom

MacBride, S., 1980. Many voices, one world (Voix multiples, un seul monde), Commission report. https://digitallibrary.un.org/record/80?ln=en

Macdowall, I., 1992. *Reuters handbook for journalists*. Oxford: Butterworth Heinemann.

Maras, S., 2013. *Objectivity in journalism*. Cambridge: Polity Press.

Mooney, B. and Simpson, B., 2003. *Breaking news: How the wheels came off at Reuters*. Chichester: Capstone Publishing Ltd.

Palmer, M., 2019. *International news agencies: A history*. Cham, Switzerland: Springer International Publishing.

Parry, R., 2011. *The ascent of media: From Gilgamesh to Google via Gutenburg*. London: Nicholas Brealey Publishing.

Paterson, C.A., 2011. *The international television news agencies: The world from London*. New York: Peter Lang.

Rantanen, T., 2009. *When news was new*. Oxford: John Wiley & Sons.

Read, D., 1992. *The power of news: The history of Reuters*. Oxford: Oxford University Press.

Thomson Reuters. 2021. Trust principles. https://www.thomsonreuters.com/en/about-us/trust-principles.html

Schudson, M., 1978. *Discovering the news—A social history of the American newspaper*. New York: Basic Books.

Schudson, M., 2001. The objectivity norm in American journalism. *Journalism*, 2(2), pp. 149–170.

Wahl-Jorgensen, K., 2013. The strategic ritual of emotionality: A case study of Pulitzer Prize-winning articles. *Journalism*, 14(1), pp. 129–145.

Williams, K., 2011. *International journalism*. London: Sage.

2 Weathering the storm
Can more than 150 years of tradition save the news agencies?

> If I have one piece of advice, it's to stay true to the Trust Principles and preserve our defining commitment to integrity, independence, and freedom from bias.
>
> Stephen Adler, former editor-in-chief, Reuters

Introduction

When Stephen Adler stepped down in April 2021 after ten years as the Editor-in-Chief of Reuters, his parting message to staff was clear – stick to the tried and tested recipe, the core values that had seen the news agency weather periodic crises of the past 170 years. The Trust Principles, drawn up in 1941,[1] are deeply ingrained in its journalistic culture and Adler, whose career had previously been spent with very different news organisations, the *Wall Street Journal* and *Businessweek*, had been keen to champion them during his years at the agency. For much of his time as the helm, Reuters and its rivals, perhaps with the sole exception of Bloomberg which has continued to expand and thrive, had been in a state of near perpetual financial strain as they struggled to cope with the disruption wrought by the advent of social media and its impact on the traditional business model of news. To make matters worse, the COVID-19 pandemic has delivered a further blow to newspapers, one of the agencies' traditional customers, and led to fundamental changes in working practices, the consequences of which are still being evaluated. Faced with such turmoil and uncertainty, the news agencies did what they have always done at such times in their history – they adapted to the changing news landscape, cut costs and reaffirmed the validity of their age-old news values of objectivity and fact-based journalism. But to what extent has that strategy worked and is it still valid? This chapter examines the

DOI: 10.4324/9781003029656-3

agencies' strategic response and explores the risks and opportunities as they adjust their business models.

In what at times appeared to be an unseemly scramble, the agencies have attempted to embrace the digital age and social media environment, seeking out new opportunities. In a sense, such a move reflects a deep-seated survival instinct, the same that kicked in when at points in history they were confronted with the challenge of radio, television and 24-hour rolling news channels. While each new medium might have been seen as a potential threat at the time, the agencies ultimately won over new outlets for their wholesale business model. But has the current headlong foray online led to a commoditisation of news and undermined the agencies' traditional wholesale market? Have they understood the implications of moving into what is for them an unfamiliar retail market for news and is it possible to set up paywalls once their product has been in the public domain for free? And does this mean that the news agencies are now comfortable adopting a more public profile implied by their presence in the consumer market or are they still more at ease acting behind the scenes?

Further questions surround what has been a decade of relentless cost cutting in the face of shrinking revenues and a squeeze on profits, caused not least because by the need to invest in new technology. What has been the impact of cuts in editorial and the retrenchment of agency staff in foreign bureaux at a time when anyone armed with a mobile phone can upload images of distant conflicts and disasters? On the one hand, it can be seen as a logical consequence of a democratisation of news gathering fostered by technological advances. But on the other hand, it is possible that some of the agencies have actually undermined one of their key strengths, namely the ability to report from faraway places where other media organisations have no presence. If the cuts are too deep, it is likely that news coverage will suffer. And there are signs that in some cases, it may be seriously draining morale among seasoned agency journalists.

When it comes to the news itself, do audiences still want "plain vanilla" fact-based journalism that allows them to make their own judgements or are they hungry for the emotionally-laden content of social media and the opinions of journalists covering the news? It can be argued that newspapers – the traditional clients of the news agencies – are relying increasingly on visual, personal and emotional stories for sales (Coward, 2013; Kitch, 2000; Wardle, 2006). Coward contends that today's media consuming audiences want real life experience, "with all details, especially all the emotions and feelings straight from the protagonists" mouths' (2013: 3). This chapter explores the strategies employed by the news agencies and attempts to chart their successes and failures.

A continual slide in earnings but is there a route to recovery?

Each of the four major agencies has been hit by periodic downturns in the global media and finance sectors over the past decade and is braced for further financial difficulties as a result of the COVID-19 pandemic. Banks have been shedding workers and office space while some – but by no means all – wholesale media clients have seen their own markets shrink. For the agencies, this has spelt even greater uncertainty but also potential opportunities as they attempt to navigate the complex shifts in media consumption driven by the pandemic, shifts that in turn drive the business of their core clients.

The 2021 Digital News Report produced by the Reuters Institute for the Study of Journalism[2] concludes that the pandemic has hastened the demise of printed newspapers in many countries, with frequent reports of lay-offs as advertisers take fright in the face of a global economic downturn. In purely practical terms, lockdowns hampered the physical distribution and stocking of newspapers, accelerating the shift to a digital future and driving further consolidation of titles. Public concerns about the risk of contamination from copies sold at newsstands affected daily sales in many countries (Newman et al., 2021: 14). But on the positive side, the Reuters Institute charts the rise of consumer news subscriptions during the pandemic and detects a new appetite for fact-based information (ibid: 10). As such, its detailed analysis provides the agencies with valuable insights on a country-by-country basis into which media sectors are benefitting during the pandemic and which are suffering (ibid):

> Television news has continued to perform strongly in some countries, but print newspapers have seen a further sharp decline almost everywhere as lockdowns impacted physical distribution, accelerating the shift towards a mostly digital future.

There are, however, further uncertainties for Reuters and Bloomberg, both of which draw the majority of their revenues from financial clients. So far, major financial institutions have been giving out mixed signals about the future of office space once working from home regimes introduced during the COVID-19 pandemic are relaxed. Trading operations, a core business for both news outlets, are unlikely to shed terminals since working from home poses serious problems in terms of banking compliance and cyber security. But for other operations, the picture is far from clear. Goldman Sachs, for example, has led the pack in demanding that its staff return to the office (*Financial Times*, 2021a). Others, such as HSBC, have stated that it plans to reduce substantially its office footprint and adopt a much more flexible policy towards home working. According to the *Financial Times*, Société Générale is among those banks taking a more "laissez-faire" approach to post-pandemic working arrangements. It plans to let most bankers work from home up to three days a week, after striking a deal with French labour unions that has become a template for all employees regardless of the country they work in (ibid). The *Financial Times* concluded that for bankers who are often out of the office seeking to win clients, advising on deals or working in back-office support functions, there is likely to be a flexible approach.

When it comes to their own financial performance, not all the agencies are transparent. All do produce annual reports and revenue data, or estimates, are generally available. But it is notoriously difficult to establish just how profitable news operations are. At Reuters and Bloomberg, this is complicated by the fact that the core business is selling data and equipment to financial markets – the media markets represent a small share of total revenue. News may be a vital component of the total package for customers of these two organisations, but there has been an unresolved debate for years on whether editorial should be viewed as a cost centre or profit centre and how to separate out the editorial spend from the rest of the organisations' business. The two agencies also have a completely different business model in that they are driven by profit – Thomson Reuters is a stock-listed company publishing quarterly earnings, while Bloomberg is privately owned. By contrast, the AP is a not-for-profit co-operative owned by US newspapers and broadcasters. Agence France-Presse (AFP) does operate as a commercial business but, despite its fiercely guarded editorial independence, the agency still receives subsidies each year from the French government.

Bloomberg has generally been able to buck the downward trend, increase its market share and project an upbeat image. It brands itself as "the global leader in business and financial data, news, and insight" (Bloomberg Philanthropies Annual Report, 2020). Today, it is estimated by Forbes to have worldwide revenues of more than $10 billion, having overtaken those of Thomson Reuters in 2012. Bloomberg's new European headquarters building, opened in London in 2017, was designed by architects Foster + Partners and cost about

£1 billion. On its opening, *The Guardian* newspaper characterised it as looking like a "regional department store" but design considerations aside, the 3.2-acre site in the heart of the City of London is testimony to Bloomberg's economic success, its emphasis on brand recognition and sheer confidence over the past decade. Bloomberg promptly won the Royal Institute of British Architects annual "Stirling" award for the UK's best new building.[3] For several years, founder Michael Bloomberg had taken a back seat in his company, first as mayor of New York from 2002 to 2013, then, more briefly in 2020, as a presidential candidate. But his name has rarely been out of the headlines as one of the America's richest men and he was on hand for the grand opening of the new headquarters building alongside London mayor Sadiq Khan.

By contrast, Reuters has seen its fortunes steadily decline. While it had ridden the crest of the dot.com wave during the 1990s, its profits started to slide as the market turned and the financial sector struggled. This led in 2008 to the £8.7 billion takeover by the Canadian Thomson Corporation but the merger has been widely seen as a failure and "a sorry tale of management upheaval, culture clashes and disappointing product launches" (Wachman, 2011). Pre-merger in 2007, Reuters could boast 36% of the global market for screen-based information compared to just 25% for Bloomberg. But today, estimates show that the Reuters share is just 23% compared to Bloomberg's 33%. The Bloomberg terminal has about 325,000 users worldwide while the terminal developed by Thomson Reuters, known as the "Eikon," has about 190,000. Shares in the newly merged Thomson Reuters entity had slumped by 14% on the first day of trading in 2008, with staff threatening to strike over job cuts. In fact, the next years would see a series of culls (see the section in this chapter below) as Bloomberg stretched its lead in the market for financial news and data. At that time, the Reuters chief executive Tom Glocer, who took overall charge of the merged group, held out hopes that the deal would avoid the ill-fated mergers of other large tie-ups such as AOL-Time Warner and CBS-Viacom. But by the end of 2011, Glocer had been eased out by the Canadian Thomson family to be replaced by the company's Chief Operating Officer James Smith. The last senior Reuters executive had been removed from the top table. Since then, the company has been radically slimmed down, with 55% of a whole division hived off in 2018 to private equity company the Blackstone Group. The division was renamed Refinitiv and subsequently sold to the London Stock Exchange for $27 billion. Reuters News, still in the hands of Thomson Reuters, is a barely profitable unit of what is left, making up just 10.5%

of total revenue (Thomson Reuters Annual Report, 2020). One major lifeline is a deal in which it is guaranteed payments of about $325 million a year to provide news and editorial content to Refinitiv until 2048.[4] The open question, however, is whether this financial cushion, reassuring as it is, will influence the editorial output or focus it even more tightly on the needs of financial clients to the detriment of general news, video and still images.

The other two agencies, AP and AFP have been spared the headlines generated by stock market deals, share price fluctuations or stories about the political ambitions, wealth and tax affairs of Michael Bloomberg. But that is not to say that they have been shielded from the disruption to global media markets and both are more reliant on traditional print and broadcast media than Reuters and Bloomberg.

AFP was able to report a small net profit of 400,000 euros in 2019, the first time it had recorded a profit since 2013, and increased this to 5.3 million euros in 2020 (AFP, 2020). At the same time, however, AFP benefitted substantially from support from the French state of 115.5 million euros in 2020.[5] A year earlier, AFP had warned about the impact of the COVID-19 pandemic on future earnings (AFP, 2020):

> Although not yet fully felt, the inevitable impacts of the Covid-19 pandemic on AFP's core business will undoubtedly come to light over the coming months. Despite the fact that the agency's turnover is generated mainly from subscriptions, it will nevertheless be affected by the financial weakening of its media clients, the cancellation of major sporting events (particularly in the image sector), the reduction of advertising income and, of course, the various restrictions that make marketing more difficult.

AFP's reliance on a strong photo service means it has been vulnerable to the cancellation of major sporting tournaments, such as the Tokyo Olympics and European Football Championships Euro 2020, both pushed back into 2021 as a result of the pandemic. Although that had the potential to damage revenues from its AFP Services and SID[6] subsidiaries, AFP's commercial revenues did hold up in 2020 and were marginally above 2019 levels. In the final analysis, AFP was able to save costs by not having to staff major sporting events. AP's annual revenue reached a peak in 2008 at $748 million but the shift to online media and the parlous state of its owners, the US newspaper and broadcast industry, has taken its toll since, dropping to $510 million in 2017 according to the latest available figures. Some independent analyst estimates put it still lower today but the agency did not publish figures in its most recent annual reports which focus instead on editorial coverage, journalism prizes and investment in new technology and services.

Adapting to social media and the rush to digital

All the big four agencies have followed their traditional strategy of adapting to the new media landscape but with mixed results and at times, as will be discussed below, investment has come at the expense of cost cutting. The starting point for all of them has been to establish a web and social media presence and move editing, broadcast and still images into the digital age while trying to retain old customers and capture new ones. At the simplest level, the driving force has been to create a brand awareness and promote their news gathering strengths at a time when traditional media outlets have been struggling financially and shrinking. But the transition online, including the introduction of mobile phone apps displaying their news, has been far from easy, exposing inherent tensions within the news agencies and leading to a forced change in culture. For more than a century, the agencies had been content to remain in the background and promote their credentials quietly behind the scenes to financial and media subscribers. Those credentials were verified largely on the strength of their performance as news providers in terms of the timeliness and usefulness of the information. But with their news now on public display, the agencies have inevitably been sucked into the social media whirl of opinion and counter opinion, fact and fiction. The once clearly delineated boundaries between wholesale and retail markets are becoming increasingly blurred. Just how the agencies have dealt with this cultural shock and dilemmas of, for example, covering highly divisive stories such as the Trump presidency is the subject of Chapter 3. What follows here focuses more on the strategic and business considerations of the agencies' move into the digital era.

From a strategic perspective, there has been a nagging question of whether posting stories, images and video publicly online, material which had otherwise been fed on a wholesale basis to news providers on a long-term corporate subscription basis, would undermine the agencies' own business model.[7] And the news agencies have faced the question every media company has grappled with since the advent of social media – whether to introduce a paywall or not. The Reuters Institute 2021 survey suggests that strong national news brands *do* have the ability to tap into the subscription market although there is a still widespread reluctance to pay for news (Newman et al., 2021: 11):

> We have seen significant increases in payment for online news in a small number of richer Western countries, but the overall percentage of people paying for online news remains low … In most countries a large proportion of digital subscriptions go to just a few big national brands, reinforcing the winner takes most dynamics that we have reported in the past.

Certainly, the *New York Times* has flourished during the pandemic (and before that during the Trump presidency – enjoying a so-called Trump bump). It set a record for new digital-only news subscribers in 2020, adding 1.7 million during what was a momentous news year, with stories ranging from COVID-19 to the US election and the Black Lives Matter campaign. The rate of new subscriptions has since slowed, but the total now for its digital edition and print newspaper exceeds 8.0 million and the newspaper is projecting a further rise to close to 8.5 million by the end of 2021.

By adopting a subscription model at $34.99 per month, Bloomberg has also ridden the wave of increased subscriptions. It was potentially risking the cannibalisation of its core terminal revenue at financial clients. But the decision to put its news behind an online paywall in 2018 had a different logic – it aimed to open up a *new* market of subscribers interested in serious financial news but not requiring the second-by-second coverage available through the Bloomberg terminal which can cost more than $20,000 a year. Bloomberg is notoriously reluctant to publish data about its business but the number of digital subscribers is estimated to be well into six figures, with the daily increase running three times higher than normal during the early months of the pandemic (Digiday, 2020). According to the *Financial Times*, Bloomberg anticipates reaching 400,000 consumer subscribers by the end of 2021 (2021b). Typically, for the culture of Bloomberg, the move to online subscriptions has been supported by an aggressive marketing campaign called "*Inventing Possibilities*" featuring a full social media offering on channels such as YouTube and Spotify. By allowing consumers to access ten articles on the website for free each month, Bloomberg has also ensured that news searches on Google still show its news and brand. Outlining its campaign, the Bloomberg marketing team stressed how the agency aims to expand beyond its core market:[8]

The campaign's objective was to broaden the scope of Bloomberg Media. We understand that the Bloomberg audience isn't focused solely on today's market moves; they're interested in the major shifts around the world. We wanted to create awareness of Bloomberg Media's breadth of coverage beyond our core markets and finance.

According to Mark Wood, a former Editor-in-Chief at Reuters, it is a strategy that has been extremely successful and Bloomberg has the potential to increase the number of its digital subscribers significantly further without cannibalising its core financial market.

If I am buying my Bloomberg terminal, I want real-time news and I want all the best news, so they don't compete on timing," he said in an interview for this book. "But they identified a market of people willing to pay subscriptions around the world, and these are people in business ... but not real-time business.

Wood estimates that this global market of people willing to pay for high-quality business news (not in "real time") could be as large as 20 million. But the other agencies have so far not been able to emulate Bloomberg's success in instituting a paywall or tap into that potential. To make matters worse, Reuters has been embroiled in a high-profile row with Refinitiv and its owner the London Stock Exchange that has even called into question the quality of its news output. In May 2021, Reuters was forced to postpone the launch of its website paywall through which it had also planned to charge subscribers $34.99 per month (exactly the same as that charged by Bloomberg). Chief marketing officer Josh London had called the launch "the largest digital transformation at Reuters in a decade" but at the heart of the dispute is the accusation that Reuters has breached its lucrative 30-year news supply agreement with Refinitiv. The dispute represented a clear setback to the Reuters strategy of trying to build new sources of revenue but also highlighted the potential conflicts between the agencies' traditional wholesale business model and the consumer, retail-oriented culture of the online environment where for many years the expectation has been that news is free. While the Reuters.com website has attracted more than 40 million unique visitors per month, Reuters own analysis suggested that this could be split into two groups – those looking for breaking news and market professionals looking for in-depth context and analysis about their industry. The latter is exactly the market that Bloomberg has started to capture. In a note accompanying its newly redesigned home page, Reuters makes clear that it is not targeting casual consumers of news but rather decision-makers:

> From our redesigned homepage, industry verticals and article pages, we've built an immersive multimedia experience that's not only engaging, but essential for globally minded professionals ... in the weeks ahead, you'll find more actionable insights as well as a suite of tools designed to give you an edge each and every day.

The tension between wholesale and retail markets is also apparent in the agencies' public statements about their Internet reach and their rush to embrace the digital environment through mobile apps and various social media feeds including Twitter and YouTube. The ap.news.com site also registers around 40 million users per month, the majority of those in North America, while the AP's Twitter feed has more than 15 million followers. AFP has clearly seen the need to strengthen its English-language provision to keep up in the digital world and promote its global news gathering reach. It has two million followers of its Twitter feed in English and showcases its award-winning photography and link with Getty Images.

At the same time as displaying their output through diverse online platforms, the agencies have had to invest heavily in digital technology to modernise their news gathering capability and to be able to feed that news to their traditional wholesale customers. In addition to that, the COVID-19 pandemic has seen many journalists working from home and also given new impetus to technological innovation. The initial signals from the pandemic suggest that television is a potential growth market for the agencies and one that Reuters and AP are well equipped to capitalise on through its existing wholesale contracts with major broadcasters. The Reuters Institute 2021 survey is cautious about longer term trends but identifies a clear shift during periods of lockdown or other COVID-19 restrictions (Newman et al., 2021: 11):

> Across a number of European countries, we find that consumption of television news is significantly higher than a year ago when no restrictions on movement were in place. This is not surprising, given that so many people have been stuck at home, but has reaffirmed the importance of a medium that is accessible, easy to consume, reaches a wide range of demographics, and is mostly well trusted. Twenty-four-hour news channels such as Sky News (+5 percentage points) in the UK and n-tv (+6 pp) in Germany are amongst the brands to have benefited.

It is a trend that has not escaped the attention of AFP. For the past few years, AFP has been investing heavily in video formats and television news gathering, keenly aware that it had lagged behind its competitors APTN and Reuters TV in this area. What AFP calls "double-digit growth" in video was one of the drivers in a small rise in its overall commercial revenues in 2020 (AFP Annual Report) and the agency believes that it has now reached a level where it can compete on an equal footing with what had been a de facto duopoly. Its global news director Phil Chetwynd[9] wrote in the report:

> In the first six months of the pandemic, we had live television broadcasts from more than 1,500 different datelines. The feedback has been extremely positive from major television broadcasters all around the world.

Elaborating on AFP's drive into video during an interview for this book, Chetwynd said that the agency had been building its capability steadily for the last 10–15 years and had benefitted from being able to come to market with a digital video product not a legacy TV product, building this into the core of the newsroom. Over the last couple of years, AFP has added about 80–90 new video jobs. "It is a real multi-media newsroom," he said, "where everyone has to plan and think in terms of multi-media production." The challenge will be to displace contracts currently held by APTN or Reuters TV, something that might be hampered by lack of archive footage. AFP also launched in November 2020 what it calls *AFP News*, a content distribution platform which it sees as key to retaining existing clients and gaining new ones. AP has also foregrounded its investment in video and still image equipment, complicated by, but also driven by, the pandemic and need for its journalists to be able to edit and file from home and remote locations. It has also been introducing a variety of new tools, both for its journalists and clients – an updated version of its ENPS or electronic news production system which is now in 700 newsrooms worldwide, and the introduction of what it calls AP Playbook to coordinate coverage plans.

Editorial is the target for cost cutting

All this investment has come at a cost. All of the agencies, including Bloomberg, have clamped down on expenditure in the past few years and in some cases cut back substantially the number of their journalists. The question is, to what extent do cuts in editorial undermine the ability to cover the news and at what point do continued cost savings drag down morale across the organisation.

Certainly, at Reuters, a tipping point appears to have been reached which is leading to increasingly vocal criticism of cost cutting. A long history of job cuts dates back to 2003 and almost resulted in a strike during the takeover of Reuters by the Thomson Corporation in 2008. That was averted when negotiations with the UK National Union of Journalists led to an agreement that compulsory redundancies would be replaced with a voluntary scheme. In the end, about 70 UK newsroom staff accepted voluntary redundancy. Since then, in 2018, a new wave of redundancies was announced aimed at reducing the global workforce (not just editorial) by 3,200 jobs to about 23,800, together with the closure of 55 offices worldwide. Steadily but surely cuts to editorial have been implemented, reducing the total number of journalists worldwide to about 2,500 from 3,000. The cuts have hit the agency's 16 foreign language services hard, particularly those in France and Germany. Those services had provided the backbone for the English-language global reporting network, often covering local press conferences and generating stories which might otherwise not have been covered by foreign correspondents on assignment to the country. The French newspaper *Le Monde*, commenting on particularly deep cuts to the French-language desk in Paris, where staffing has been almost halved since 2010, talked about a "deep malaise" among staff (*Le Monde*, 2021). The newspaper cited a policy of cutting costs in established global news centres such as Paris and effectively outsourcing coverage to cheaper cities such as Gdansk in Poland and Bangalore in India. It quoted one Paris union official, Patrick Vignal, as saying most of those employed in Poland had no training in journalism and some did not even have a command of the French language. It was, he said, a catastrophe. *Le Monde* described the Reuters news agency business as lost within the giant Thomson Reuters group, for which it represented just a footnote and indeed one which is far less profitable than other parts of the business. The most disturbing charge is that these cuts are harming the actual news gathering. When the Suez Canal was blocked for six days in March 2021, Reuters was way behind Bloomberg on breaking one of the most important news stories of the year, critical because of the implications for the disruption to global trade and finance. Estimates of the delay across rival agencies range between five hours and six minutes. But in the financial and commodity markets, six minutes is a lifetime. The policy of outsourcing some basic news gathering to centres such as Bangalore is not new. It clearly makes sense for routine company announcements, whether in London, New York or San Francisco, to be handled outside main editorial centres where journalists can focus on covering news conferences and analysing company performance. But some Reuters journalists feel that in the drive to cut costs, the process has gone far further than expected, leaving holes in basic news coverage.

Critics of Reuters, including many of its senior journalists who have left the company in the past few years, also believe its editorial leadership has pursued a false strategy of investing too much money and effort into long-form, investigative journalism in an attempt to win a prestigious Pulitzer prize – something it had never done in almost a century of such awards.[10] Insiders attribute this to Adler's background of previous employment as a journalist at the *Wall Street Journal* and the Editor-in-Chief of *Businessweek* and maintain that the agency has taken its eye off the ball and neglected the core business of fast, accurate breaking news. Over the past ten years, while cutting costs elsewhere, Reuters hired a number of high-profile US editors and writers with a history of winning Pulitzer prizes for written work to complement its success in photography awards.[11] And it has indeed in the past few years won a series of Pulitzer Prizes. In 2014, journalists Jason Szep and Andrew Marshall won the International category for "their courageous reports on the violent persecution of the Rohingya, a Muslim minority in Myanmar that, in efforts to flee the country, often falls victim to predatory human-trafficking networks." In 2018, Clare Baldwin, Andrew Marshall and Manuel Mogato were also rewarded for what the prize committee said was "relentless reporting that exposed the brutal killing campaign behind Philippines President Rodrigo Duterte's war on drugs." In 2019, Reuters won the International Affairs award for its reporting from Myanmar (which had seen journalists Wa Lone and Kyaw Soe Oo imprisoned for more than 500 days and an international campaign for their release). And in 2021, Andrew Chung, Lawrence Hurley, Andrea Januta, Jaimi Dowdell and Jackie Botts shared the prize for explanatory reporting with *The Atlantic* for their examination of the obscure US legal doctrine of "qualified immunity" and how it can shield police who use excessive force from prosecution. The immense pride in such awards and courageous journalism is, however, balanced by concerns that a priority placed on long-form stories and prizes, combined with editorial cuts, means the agency is losing its competitive edge in financial news. Concern in the organisation was such that a "speed week" was held to reinforce the need to be first with breaking news.

AFP for its part announced a "transformation plan" in October 2018 aimed at saving 14 million euros on wages and a further 5 million euros in other costs by 2023. Such savings have meant not replacing staff who are retiring and reducing the terms and conditions of expatriate staff. The total net reduction of staff aimed at by AFP management has been stated publicly at 95 posts, of which 23 are in editorial (although the addition of video staff and those working in areas of verification has since resulted in a net increase). An editorial reorganisation in Paris, bringing two editorial sites into one, aims to generate annual savings of 2.5 million euros and create a more modern integrated newsroom. But the local union, SUD-AFP[12], has been vocal in criticising reorganisation plans and working conditions in Paris. Despite its brash public image and its strong market share against Reuters, Bloomberg has not been immune and also announced up to 90 editorial job cuts during the pandemic although this appeared to be part of a rebalancing of its news team. The move included senior editors in Europe as part of a global restructuring of its media division (*Financial Times*, 2021b). Bloomberg Editor John Micklethwait was reported to have told staff in a memo that the logic was to streamline editing while the organisation would continue to invest in data journalism, planning to end 2021 with the same number of journalists as it had before the pandemic. An internal memo from Micklethwait set out the plan to slim down and speed up editing, cutting back on duplication:

> For the most part, we will stick to the principle of one story, one editor. No more unnecessary back-reading or re-editing. Yes, of course there will be more complicated pieces that require senior managers to be involved, but those are the exceptions. We either trust an editor to handle a story, or we don't. If we don't like the end result, we give the editor candid feedback.

Micklethwait said that the newsroom needed more "ownership and accountability," pointing to cases where Bloomberg had moved too slowly to break a news story.

For its part, AP has been feeling the long-running downturn in US newspapers which make up a major part of its co-operative ownership structure and had announced a round of 25 editorial layoffs in 2016. According to the Poynter Institute for Media Studies about 1,800 US newspapers have closed since 2004, with 70 of those closures coming during the pandemic. Cost cutting has focused on AP's network of international bureaux which has been slimmed down considerably. Bureaux have been closed, the generous "ex-pat" packages for correspondents on assignment from the United States have been phased out, leading to a reliance on cheaper local journalists and stringers.

Expatriate packages typically comprised a base salary, housing allowance, health benefits, education costs for children to attend school and airline tickets back home every year or every second year. It is hardly a surprise then that AP's US newspaper and broadcast members, at a time of intense financial pressure, should be more interested in its offering of domestic news than that from a costly network of foreign bureaux. But much as is the case with Reuters, critics are asking whether the cuts have gone too far and will undermine the AP's reputation for its global reach. In analysing AP's shrinking global footprint, the Columbia Journalism Review (CJR) stated bluntly that the agency's nickname of being "the Marine Corps of Journalism" (meaning always first in and last out) simply no longer applied (Frazier, 2019). The counter argument, posited by AP editorial management, is that by ending the two-tier system of expatriate and local staff, AP will be drawing on more local expertise and opening up opportunities for local journalists. Outgoing executive editor Sally Buzbee was quoted by CJR as saying local journalists were emerging as AP's "most vibrant and forward-looking correspondents." She added:

> Twenty years ago, we would have a white guy heading our Mideast operations, now we have a woman. We are trying to be more modern in our staffing.
>
> I get a little prickly that someone in the US thinks they should have a salary out of whack with the very talented people in the country where they are working. It doesn't make sense for me to take an American, or plop a journalist with a generous salary in a foreign bureau. We have had an unequal system. It benefits the people who got expat packages, and suppresses the talent of those who didn't. I admit it might be unfair for the people who aren't getting expat packages anymore, but it was a two-tier system.

The shift in policy also goes some way to countering the Western centric viewpoint of foreign correspondents. Debating the pros and cons of the move, the CJR commented:

> For decades, the AP has been criticized for a colonialist reporting model, with well-paid, often Ivy League-educated reporters parachuting in to filter local events, and especially America's many wars, through a uniquely Western lens. Meanwhile, local fixers, translators and stringers, who helped expat correspondents do their jobs, earned far less, with little status or influence over the narratives told about their countries.

Who wants plain vanilla news?

Faced with such financial pressures, the news agencies have also sought to go on the offensive by drawing on their long tradition – and basic instinct – of delivering fact-based news. There are signs that what seemed to have been going out of fashion, and denigrated through social media channels as being rooted in the establishment and simply too dull, is experiencing a comeback. The change had been visible in the United Kingdom during the acrimonious referendum to leave the European Union and during the Trump presidency in the United States. The global COVID-19 crisis has tended to reinforce a distrust in social media, and news agencies have seen an opportunity to promote their credentials as purveyors of unbiased, "plain-vanilla" news without the spin. As the Reuters Institute states in its 2021 Digital News Report (Newman et al., 2021: 10):

> This crisis has ... shown the value of accurate and reliable information at a time when lives are at stake. In many countries we see audiences turning to trusted brands – in addition to ascribing a greater confidence in the media in general. The gap between the "best and the rest" has grown, as has the trust gap between the news media and social media ...
> It would be wrong to over-emphasise any temporary bump in TV consumption given the longer-term shift towards digital sources but it is a reminder of the continuing draw of video-based storytelling as well as the strength of traditional news brands. But perhaps the most striking finding around consumption has been the extent to which people have placed a premium on reliable news sources in general, not just on TV.

The backlash against news on social media is also, of course, inextricably linked to the debate over "fake news" which once again came to the fore as former president Trump refused to acknowledge the outcome of the 2020 US election and with the storming of the US Capitol in January 2021. Despite what at times appears to be an ever growing polarisation of politics, the Reuters Institute detects there is a silent majority which perceives a growing trust gap between the news of traditional brands they rely on and the news they find on social media.

Traditional public service broadcasters such as the BBC have experienced growing audiences for their main news bulletins and, as noted above, other trusted brands such as the *New York Times* have been able to increase subscriptions. Nor has this gone unnoticed at the news agencies which have without exception used their social media channels to underscore their ethos of fact-based news and long history of fact-checking. The AP states on its main news website that is dedicated to factual reporting and that it "remains the most trusted source of fast, accurate, unbiased news in all formats and the essential provider of the technology and services vital to the news business." In common with others, Reuters emphasises that it provides news which allows its customers to make decisions rather than giving its own views, stating it provides: "Everything you need to make smarter and faster decisions…" AFP draws on the combination of speed and accuracy, saying it provides "fast, comprehensive and verified coverage of the events shaping our world and of the issues affecting our daily lives" Its 2020 annual report is called "Facts Matter." Bloomberg also underscores the message that is providing the basis for independent decision-making rather than telling customers what to think. It states: "Global customers rely on us to deliver accurate, real-time business and market-moving information that helps them make critical financial decisions."

At the same time, the news agencies have capitalised on the concern around fake news to explore the business opportunities afforded by fact-checking. Since the emergence of Factcheck.org[13] in the United States in 2003, fact-checking operations have expanded globally (Amazeen, 2020: 95). The Duke Reporters Lab, a journalism research centre at Duke University, keeps a tally of active verification sites worldwide, with the number expanding to around 340 in 2021 from 100 in 2016 (in addition, 112 sites are currently listed as inactive). AFP has built up what is calls a "digital verification network" with more than 100 journalists covering 80 countries to bolster its fact-checking but also sees this, alongside video, as a driver for revenue growth. The agency has launched what it calls "AFP Fact Check" on a monthly subscription basis starting from $500 per month. In a similar fashion, Reuters has made verification into a business service in addition to its routine editorial operation. Both agencies are now offering training courses on verification and media literacy and working with Facebook. The Reuters fact-checking unit struck a deal with Facebook in 2020, verifying content posted by users in the United States and United Kingdom on Facebook and its subsidiary Instagram. AFP most recently added a German language team to its series of agreements with the social media organisation and has verification deals in the works with TikTok and others. AP has a dedicated fact-check website, posting stories in which its journalists have investigated claims. Describing its operation and the site, AP says:

> When a public figure says something questionable, it is our job to investigate it and offer the facts … In addition, when a false story

gains traction online, we create a separate fact-checking item that tells the true story.

Just how these fact-checking operations work in practice is discussed in detail in the next chapter but it is clear that strategically the news agencies have spotted the business opportunity to leverage their core strength in verification to offer a much needed outsourced service to social media platforms who are keen to demonstrate they are taking the threat of fake news seriously (and who are keen to stave off statutory regulation).

Conclusion

At one time, it appeared that two decades of decline in the news agencies' traditional newspaper and broadcast clients might be irreversible. But the COVID-19 pandemic, for all the human suffering and chaos it has brought to the global economy, may in a perverse and unexpected way be changing that picture. As the Reuters Institute observes, the pandemic has indeed driven another nail into the coffin of print media, with some newspaper buyers even nervous about picking up a piece of paper for fear of contracting the virus (Newman et al., 2021: 14). But on the other hand, broadcasters have seen a resurgence in viewing figures and renewed trust in their public service role as providers of fact-based information. It is admittedly unclear whether this will be a lasting trend, but it does spell a business opportunity for the news agencies as they seek to adapt to the digital media landscape – television and image-driven output is likely to be key to future revenue growth in their media business. AFP's editorial strategy and decisive move into digital video content clearly illustrates this.

As for financial clients, it remains to be seen whether banks will shed office space – and with it Reuters and Bloomberg terminals – and migrate some of their operations to home working. The agencies can anticipate being able to protect their core revenue from trading terminals where a closely monitored, secure office environment is required for reasons of banking regulation and compliance. But some major banks are seeking to slim down their office space and seize the chance to cut costs. In the meantime, both Reuters and Bloomberg are keen to tap into a potentially large market of business professionals who are ready to pay a subscription fee for specialist financial news that foregoes the (much more expensive) second-by-second real-time alerts provided for traders.

At the same time, the agencies have demonstrated their ability to keep a lid on costs and tried to promote a role of trusted fact-checkers at a time of endemic disinformation on social media. While this chapter has explored the news agencies' business strategies related to fact-based journalism, Chapter 3 examines in detail what their long tradition and deeply ingrained ethos means in terms of the actual *practice* of journalism in newsrooms and in the field. How have they deployed their journalists to engage in fact-checking and how have they handled the politically sensitive stories of the Trump presidency and the COVID-19 pandemic? How have they managed the tensions between the public's hunger for emotionally driven news and reliable information? And how are their journalists expected to behave on social media when platforms such as Twitter and Facebook are also used for breaking news?

Notes

1. See Chapter 1, p. 23.
2. The report is based on a survey of more than 92,000 people from 46 markets around the world, including for the first time India, Indonesia, Thailand, Nigeria, Colombia and Peru.
3. Reuters received a similarly mixed reception when it built a new US headquarters at 3 Times Square in New York. The 30-storey building, which opened in May 2001, was favourably reviewed in some quarters but *Architecture* magazine (Cramer, 2000) said: "What they built is more of an identity crisis—a mish-mash of forms and materials utterly lacking in finesse or wit or higher meaning."
4. $336 million revenue was booked in each of the years 2019 and 2020.
5. The European Union ruled in a competition case in 2014 that AFP could keep its state funding for the time being but must comply with EU competition rules. A complaint had been brought by a now defunct German news agency four years earlier. The ruling said any funding from the French state had to be justified by public service missions.
6. AFP's German subsidiary Sport-Informations-Dienst provides multi-media sports coverage in text, image and video formats, along with live results, athlete profiles and analysis.
7. The European Alliance of News Agencies, which groups national news agencies but also includes AFP, has changed the definition of the agencies' activity from simply wholesalers of news. They state that they are "Providers of news stories and also of pictures, graphics, radio and video reports and other information to both traditional media and new media environments created by the rapid development of modern information technology." See: https://www.newsalliance.org/a
8. See: https://shortyawards.com/13th/inventing-possibilities
9. Chetwynd, appointed in 2019, is the first non-French national to hold the key editorial position at AFP.
10. The Pulitzer Prizes were established in 1917 in the provisions of the will of the American newspaper publisher Joseph Pulitzer. They are administered by Columbia University in New York.

11. Reuters photographers won Pulitzers in 2008, 2016, 2018, 2019 and 2020.
12. Solidaires-Unitaires-Démocratiques à l'Agence France-Presse.
13. Factcheck.org is a non-profit website and project of the Annenberg Public Policy Center.

References

Agence France-Presse. 2020. Annual report. https://view.afp.com/2020-annual-report/home-page/p/1

Amazeen, M.A., 2020. Journalistic interventions: The structural factors affecting the global emergence of fact-checking. *Journalism*, *21*(1), pp. 95–111.

Cramer, N., 2000. Frankenstein takes Manhattan. *Architecture*, *89*(11), p. 162.

Bloomberg Philanthropies. 2020. Annual report. https://annualreport.bloomberg.org/

Frazier, M., 2019. Rethinking foreign reporting at the AP. *Columbia Journalism Review*, 19 February 2019. https://www.cjr.org/business_of_news/the-associated-press-foreign-reporting.php

Coward, R., 2013. *Speaking personally: The rise of subjective and confessional journalism*. Basingstoke: Palgrave Macmillan.

Digiday, 2020. Bloomberg Media aims to grow its six-figure subscriber base through new OTT campaign. https://digiday.com/media/bloomberg-aims-to-grow-its-six-figure-subscriber-base-through-new-ott-campaign/

Financial Times, 2021a. Global banks adopt markedly different back-to-work policies. *Financial Times*, 15 June 2021. https://www.ft.com/content/5e7761ee-b7a2-48f2-9226-fe20277c2498

Financial Times, 2021b. Bloomberg News to lay off about 90 editorial employees. *Financial Times*, 11 February 2021. https://www.ft.com/content/e1b4b258-f321-4663-b94f-abb6e6ab7623

Kitch, C., 2000. A news of feeling as well as fact: Mourning and memorial in American newsmagazines. *Journalism*, *1*(2), pp. 171–195.

Le Monde, 2021. Alessandra Galloni, nouvelle rédactrice en chef d'une agence Reuters en plein malaise. *Le Monde*, 9 June 2021. https://www.lemonde.fr/economie/article/2021/06/09/alessandra-galloni-nouvelle-redactrice-en-chef-d-une-agence-reuters-en-plein-malaise_6083388_3234.html

Newman, N., Fletcher, R., Schulz, A., Andi, S., Robertson, C.T. and Nielsen, R.K., 2021. Reuters Institute Digital News Report 2021. *Reuters Institute for the Study of Journalism*.

Thomson Reuters Annual Report, 2020. https://ir.thomsonreuters.com/financial-information/annual-reports

Wachman, R., 2011. Thomson Reuters merger hasn't lived up to expectations. 7 December 2011, *The Guardian*. https://www.theguardian.com/media/blog/2011/dec/07/thomson-reuters-merger-failings

Wardle, C., 2006. It could happen to you: The move towards "personal" and "societal" narratives in newspaper coverage of child murder, 1930–2000. *Journalism Studies*, *7*(4), pp. 515–533.

3 Back to the future
Social media, fact-checking and plain vanilla journalism

> This pandemic has revealed the sheer scale of misinformation, what I call the alternative media ecosystem. There was a tsunami of fake news over the coronavirus. It has been complicated from a scientific perspective but has also been a very sensitive topic to deal with from a political standpoint, all around the world. It is a mixture of many things, a lot of conspiracy theories stemming from a lot of mistrust in governments, authorities and official sources.
>
> Phil Chetwynd, AFP Global News Director, 2020

Introduction

In the last decade, the volume of fake news circulating via social media has reached tsunami-like proportions, infusing and at times corrupting public discourse around major sagas, such as Brexit, the Trump presidency and the COVID-19 pandemic. As Agence France-Presse's (AFP) Global News Director Phil Chetwynd pointedly observes, it can be argued that we are witnessing the emergence of an alternative media ecosystem where the sheer scale of fake news and conspiracy theories combine to undermine trust in the institutions of a liberal democracy, including established media outlets.

In theory, at least, the world's biggest news agencies, for whom fact-based reporting has been second nature since their emergence in the 19th century, should be ideally placed to counter this wave of fake news and lay down a marker for what is true and what is false. From their earliest days, they have been relied on to cast true light on complex foreign news stories, often in faraway places; and in more recent years, with their increased focus on financial journalism, they have become essential to traders as markets are buffeted by rumours. Indeed, as Chapter 2 discussed, the news agencies have been quick to promote their credentials as purveyors of plain vanilla, fact-based journalism

DOI: 10.4324/9781003029656-4

and to market their fact-checking operations. But how well placed are the agencies to play this role in practice, how successful have they been to rising to the new challenges and what are the pitfalls? This chapter explores the news agencies' uneasy relationship with social media as age-old journalistic norms of objectivity are challenged and eroded. It examines the agencies' approach to fact-checking and the dilemmas faced when handling sensitive and polarising stories such as the Trump presidency. Suddenly, the news agencies that for more than a century had acted quietly behind the scenes are being thrust into the spotlight and subjected to closer public scrutiny than ever before.

While fact-checking and fact-based journalism are deeply rooted in news agencies' ethos, social media is not and the last decade has constituted a veritable culture shock. Within that short space of time, social media has become an indispensable news gathering tool for journalism of all flavours, from muckraking and celebrity gossip to the agencies' staple diet of hard, breaking news. But the influence of social media on modern journalism goes way beyond this basic level of practice. It has diluted established media's monopoly on information, called into question concepts of gatekeeping and undermined the once deeply seated belief in the need for "objective" reporting. The challenges therefore extend deep into the culture of the news agencies for where their journalists once worked in discrete anonymity, they are today, like it or not, often expected to develop their personal "brand" and promote their stories through social media platforms such as Twitter.

Put simply, news agencies cannot avoid the tentacles of social media and have little choice but to face the challenges, and opportunities, head on. As Griessner observes (2012: 33):

> For news agencies there seems to be no way around social media – whether to use it as a news source, to connect with the audience, clients and experts, to share information about new developments and services within the company or simply to distribute stories, images or videos ...

Fact-checking takes on new dimensions

It had of course started with a burst of optimism as the democratising effect of social media was celebrated in the early years of the new millennium. Although the news events were of devastating and tragic proportions, the "Boxing Day tsunami" of 2004 and the July 7 London bombings the next year marked the moment when news organisations realised that ordinary citizens, caught up in such events, could deliver valuable content from their own mobile phones. Holidaymakers captured the moment the tidal waves struck coastal villages after the Indian Ocean earthquake and passengers trapped in bombed carriages of the London Underground transport system sent in grainy images of the devastation while broadcast news teams could not gain access. The BBC was one of the first to respond to the increasing volume of user-generated content, something that we today take for granted. Helen Boaden, who was the BBC's Director of News at the time of the London bombings, identified the attacks as a watershed and "the point at which the BBC knew that news gathering had changed forever" (2008). In a reflection on the changing news landscape and July 7, she wrote:

> Within 24 hours, the BBC had received 1,000 stills and videos, 3,000 texts and 20,000 e-mails. What an incredible resource. 24-hour television was sustained as never before by contributions from the audience; one piece on the Six O'clock News was produced entirely from pieces of user-generated content. At the BBC, we knew then that we had to change. We would need to review our ability to ingest this kind of material and our editorial policies to take account of these new forms of output.

The BBC was one of the first major news organisations to set up a user-generated content "hub," acting shortly after the London bombings. Fears at the time by senior BBC news executives that social media would undermine the BBC's code of accuracy, impartiality and objectivity were put to one side after the bombings revealed the value of material from the public (Belair-Gagnon, 2015). They would, however, as discussed later in this chapter, pose an increasingly problematic dilemma for organisations, such as the BBC and the major news agencies which quickly followed by setting up operations to monitor and "copy taste" user-generated content through such hubs. As Singer observes (2015: 26), by the mid-2000s journalists were starting to recognise its value and the boundaries around content were becoming more porous. Although such content may not conform to some normative values, it was seen as contributing to other goals, most notably a diversity of information and of information sources. Journalists' response shifted, she argues, from disapprobation to accommodation (ibid).

But a darker side emerged very quickly. User-generated content rapidly became a vehicle for the distribution of graphic and grisly images, often from conflict zones or terror attacks. While this may have at times been useful news content, it suddenly exposed journalists monitoring material to a source of traumatic stress in what had previously been considered a safe newsroom environment. It was quickly labelled the "digital frontline" (Eyewitness Media Hub, 2015: 16), In addition, the sheer volume of misinformation expanded exponentially. This in turn spawned a new industry of independent fact-checking organisations outside the mainstream news organisations. Independent attempts at verification and fact-checking can in fact be traced back at least to the early 20th century in the United States when journalists had set about investigating and challenging the claims of patent medicine producers (Amazeen, 2020: 97). The focus on growing political misinformation had gained pace during the 1990s, leading to the emergence of web-based fact-checkers such as Factcheck.org in 2003 (ibid) and the subsequent rapid expansion of similar organisations which today number as many as 340.[1] The growth in activity has been perceived as a democracy-building tool at a time when democratic institutions are thought to be weak or under threat (Amazeen, 2020: 99).

But in today's social media landscape the phrase fact-checking takes in a diverse range of activities that defies easy categorisation (Graves & Cherubini, 2016: 8). While most operations focus on investigating political claims, several also target the news media themselves, with fact-checkers made up not only from the ranks of journalism but also from the political sciences, economics, law, public policy and various forms of activism (ibid). Graves and Cherubini divide fact-checking into three categories: reporters, reformers and experts. The first, often housed in mainstream news organisations (a "newsroom model"), define their aims in journalistic terms as a vehicle to inform the public accurately and to hold politicians to account (thus citing classic normative definitions of journalism). These fact-checkers are often wary of any activist spirit sometimes associated with the activity. As will be seen below, the operations set up at the major news agencies clearly fall under this *reporter* category. The second group of *reformers* understands fact-checking primarily in activist terms and may be aiming for specific policy changes; the third category, experts, tend to position themselves within a complex area of public policy and see their role as akin to a think-tank rather than journalism.

The growth of fact-checking, both in the newsroom model and in the shape of independent organisations, comes at a time when the very nature of news in the social media age is changing, where opinion, advocacy and emotion – once frowned on in many areas of mainstream journalism – is today not only accepted by audiences but expected. Emotional journalism (e.g. sensationalist tabloid journalism) was often labelled "bad" journalism (Zelizer, 2000: ix) as a consensual occupational ideology and value system based on objectivity was firmly established among journalists (Deuze, 2005: 3). But with the advent of social media and digital platforms, the use of emotive content in news has broken into the open and journalism's regime of emotional containment has finally broken down (Jukes, 2020: 160). Citizens who are caught up in the news and capture the action on a mobile phone – sometimes called "accidental journalists" (Allan, 2014) – have no allegiance to objective reporting; journalists are encouraged to express themselves on social media platforms such as Twitter and are more likely to cultivate a personal brand (Molyneux, Holton, & Lewis, 2018: 1386). Nowhere is this clearer to see than with the so-called Foxification of news, in which mainstream broadcasters such as Fox in the United States or the newly launched GB News in the United Kingdom advertise their content as being a corrective to what they see as the liberal and metropolitan bias of established media. GB News, which launched in June 2021, has been characterised as a "non-stop, opinionated, US-style "anti-woke" current affairs television channel aimed at a British audience" (Waterson, 2021). All this increases the pressure on established producers of fact-based news which place an emphasis on norms of objectivity and impartiality, representing all sides of an argument and allowing audiences to draw their own conclusions about events. Such developments have left the news agencies caught in the crossfire of the culture wars between mainstream news providers such as the BBC or *New York Times* and opinion-led newcomers railing against the liberal elite.

On the one hand, the news agencies cannot ignore social media, they depend on it for content, distribution and marketing, and have clearly recognised the opportunity to underscore their credentials as standard bearers for fact-based journalism. Signs of a backlash against opinion-based news appear to be working in their favour. According to the Reuters Institute for the Study of Journalism's 2021 survey of news consumption, the public in many countries still strongly supports the ideals of impartial and objective news (albeit recognising that they themselves are sometimes drawn to more opinionated and less balanced content) (Newman et al., 2021: 20). An overwhelming 74% of survey respondents said news outlets should reflect a range of different views and leave it up to people to decide while only 15% felt news outlets should argue for the views they think best.[2] The survey also found, however, that younger groups are slightly less attached to impartial or neutral news, especially in the case of some burning issues of social justice. This prompts the question of whether concepts around objectivity and impartiality need rethinking to take account of changing consumer expectations as well as how journalists should conduct themselves in more informal settings such as social media and podcasts (ibid).

On the other hand, the news agencies are wary of public scrutiny, of being sucked into polarising debates and that their journalists might step out of line on social media and embroil them in political controversy at a time when politics and other sensitive subjects, not least the COVID-19 pandemic, can at any minute spark a "Twitter storm." By incorporating material from user-generated content into their own news gathering, news agencies are effectively validating that material and, at the same time, exposing their own reputation if it turns out to have been manipulated or false.

The choice between the two extremes of an opinion-based and fact-based approach to news was spelt out succinctly by the Reuters Institute in its 2021 report (29):

> In an era where news consumption has become more abundant, more fragmented, and more fractious, media companies face a choice. They can try to build a deeper relationship with a specific audience or demographic – representing and reflecting their views and aspirations. This journalism may need to take a clearer "point of view" but could also build deep trust with that specific group. On the other hand, media companies could choose to try to bridge these divides with services that work for the largest number of people possible – something much of the public say they want. In this case, the challenge will be whether journalism that balances different points of view can engage audiences sufficiently but also avoid getting caught up in the partisan and cultural battles that have been such a feature of the last few years.

Fact-checking in practice

Given their ethos for fact-based reporting, the news agencies – as set out in Chapter 2 – were only ever going to make one choice. Typical of this view are the comments of Jane Barrett, the Reuters global editor for Media News Strategy who is clear that the disintermediation of traditional media is now a fact of life, has changed age-old business models and that the clock cannot be turned back.[3]

> Social media has levelled the field of communication ... that means there are opinions out there left, right and centre from educated

musings to mad uncle Bob to dangerous and coordinated conspiracy theories. So, the need to cut through with factual reporting is the highest I have ever known it in my career.

Because of this, all the major news agencies now have operations dedicated to fact-checking over and above their traditional editing desks. These operations have often grown out of the social media monitoring hubs that were put in place in the wake of the Asian tsunami and 2005 London bombings but have been given new impetus by the flood of false information circulating during the COVID-19 pandemic. Reuters, which has joined Facebook's third-party fact-checking programme in the United Kingdom,[4] has a specialised unit whose principal aims are to "fact-check visual material and claims posted on social media." Hazel Baker, Reuters Head of user-generated content news gathering said (Reuters, 2021a):

> As the world faces up to the severity of the coronavirus outbreak, the need to stem the flow of misinformation has never been more critical. The Reuters Fact Check team is examining social media content closely in order to track viral claims made by users in the US and now also in the UK. By verifying or debunking these claims, we hope to play our role, aimed at the public's interest, in reducing the rate at which inaccurate and potentially harmful posts are being shared at this time.

In discussing its methodology, the Reuters unit applies a range of criteria to material (2021b):

- Editorial value: is the topic timely and of public interest?
- Could the material potentially cause real-world harm, if it is inaccurate?
- Reach: how far has the claim travelled? We examine the level of interactions on individual posts, as well as the visibility of the claim across different platforms.
- Potential reach: is the information likely to be shared further? We examine how quickly the post is generating interaction and consider whether it may be repeated by others.
- Balance of fact vs opinion: is it possible to isolate certain claims from the material?

In common with some of the other agencies, Reuters then posts the results of its fact-checking on its main website in story form. The first paragraph of one such story, debunking claims falsely attributed to the US immunologist Anthony Fauci, ran as follows:

> *Fact Check – Fauci did not say COVID-19 vaccines are spreading disease*
> Social media users are sharing an article that falsely claims top U.S. infectious disease official Dr Anthony Fauci said that COVID-19 vaccines are spreading the disease. The headline implies that the vaccine itself is causing the spread of the virus, *which is false*.[5] In reality, Fauci said that vaccinated people with breakthrough infections of the Delta variant show a similar level of virus in the nasopharynx as the unvaccinated cases.

The story at AFP is similar, with its collaboration with Facebook now taking in fact-checking of material in 16 languages (AFP Press Release, 2020). AFP launched what it calls its "digital investigation unit" in 2017 and has more than 100 journalists dedicated to investigating online content posting to an AFP Fact Check website. Chetwynd argues that the value of such operations both supports the fight against disinformation and has reputational benefits (AFP Annual Report, 2020: 8). He says:

> Facts do matter. Fact-checking is so complementary to, so intertwined with, our core breaking news journalism. We are all able to witness how these alternative ideas have an impact on our society ...
> Our growing fact-checking teams around the world – more than a hundred people working in multiple languages – have been a great help. It was a challenge to build this team on the front line of information but we now see the fruits of our hard work. The pandemic has given a great visibility with regards to digital verification, and it has proved very important in boosting our image as a trustworthy global news provider. It showed our customers and the public how important our work is.

Discussing APF's operation further in an interview, Chetwynd points out the benefits and cross-fertilisation of such activities within the newsroom and of efforts to integrate fact-checking and news teams. In addition, he sees such operations as important for journalism as social media platforms begin to take more seriously fact-based reporting and show increased appetite for tackling the damage that can be caused by fake news:

These are enormous platforms of information, it is where people read their journalism, it is where journalism is consumed ... to try to stay out of that a) is just impossible and b) is naïve. What we have to do, is we have to get in there, get in there and do our best to spread the message of fact-driven journalism.

There is a long way to go but you have to be pleased at least that we are getting our foot in the door; these platforms are starting to have discussions about fact-based journalism and how they can promote it ... this is existential for some of them, they really have to get on top of this ... they are all looking for solutions and that has got to be going in the right direction for journalism.

Unsurprisingly, AP also has its dedicated Fact Check website and compiles a weekly dossier of false stories in what it calls a roundup of "some of the most popular but completely untrue stories and visuals" that had been widely shared on social media. In a commonly followed format, AP journalists state the claim and then present in detail the facts. The AP team has a dedicated "Fact Check and Misinformation Editor" and body of staff. Illustrating their common policy approach, the agencies are members of the International Fact-Checking Network set up in 2015 under the auspices of the Florida-based Poynter Institute for Media Studies.[6] The IFCN's aim is to share best practice in fact-checking, promoting common standards through a code of principles[7] and offering training. Emphasising its commitment to the practice, Bloomberg put out a video shortly after the January 6, 2021 Capitol riots in Washington DC advising viewers how to spot dis- and misinformation.

Still gatekeeping or "gatewatching"?

It is one matter to verify stories circulating on social media platforms and to post an account standing up or knocking down claims. But news agencies also frequently use user-generated content for their own reporting, presenting a subtly different set of dilemmas and posing the question of whether their century-old role as gatekeepers[8] – the source of their power in setting and framing the global news agenda – is being diluted and whether they are unwittingly undermining their credentials as purveyors of plain vanilla news.

It was very quickly clear that the user-generated content that emerged from the 2004 Asian tsunami and London bombings the next year did not represent isolated occurrences. Both epitomised unforeseen incidents where no journalists and cameramen were present and where the story quickly came to dominate the headlines. By the time of the Boston marathon bombing in 2013, the incorporation of user-generated content into mainstream news reporting had become routine for all news outlets, whether hard news agencies or those organisations with a particular political viewpoint. In fact, not to use footage during such breaking news stories would today strike journalists and audiences alike as highly unusual. All news organisations recognise, of course, the value of being able to use key content they would otherwise not have (because they were not on the scene to witness it at first hand) and the immediacy of such material. But there is also another dimension to mobile phone images of, for example, terror attacks taken by citizens caught up in events. The fact that such images are *not* edited or digitally enhanced can make the impersonal detachment of mainstream news photography and journalism's preferred framing seem outmoded (Allan, 2014: 146). In this sense, such material is considered by the public to be "more real and less packaged" adding drama and human emotion to an otherwise dry news environment (Williams, Wahl-Jorgensen, & Wardle, 2011). For popular news sites such as, in the United Kingdom, the MailOnline, such content is gold dust as the economics of attention and the raw power of images come into play – emotion is leveraged to generate attention and viewing time on social media, in turn generating advertising revenue (Bakir & McStay, 2018: 155). But for news agencies, such content, if not handled with care, can risk taking on the nature of entertainment more associated with populist news outlets. The UK regulator Ofcom identified in a 2018 report on changing patterns of news consumption how news – partly because of social media platforms – is taking on characteristics of entertainment and how lines are being blurred. In the report, *Scrolling News: The Changing Face of News Consumption*, Ofcom noted how the primary source of news for many people is now the mobile phone and that this can engender a "social media mindset" (2018: 39).

That aside, the agencies, in particular, have another reason for relying on third-party content that reflects both the financial strains of the past years discussed in Chapter 2 and advances in mobile technology. The agencies' staple diet of foreign news reporting has become increasingly difficult to deliver as bureaux are slimmed down, or even closed, and the number of foreign correspondents is cut. As Sambrook observes (2010: 25):

> From the 1980s onwards there has been a relentless paring back of international resources by Western news organisations in the face of budget cuts forced by declining revenues, the need for

investment in digital technology and the demands of corporate shareholders.

Put simply, local journalists can often report the news without an agency going to the formidable expense of posting a foreign correspondent to a distant country for three years and incurring the costs of housing and healthcare, to name just a few of the benefits that used to be considered standard. Today, as AP has demonstrated as it slims down overseas bureau and ex-pat packages, that model of foreign correspondent remuneration hardly still exists but, more importantly, technological advances mean news video and images can be sent back to an editing desk by local journalists without the need for expensive cameras or satellite dishes and uplink facilities. Concerns about safety have also played a major role in increasing the agencies' use of local content, whether provided by locally based journalists or so-called fixers. Foreign correspondents working in a country, or those flown in at short notice to cover a big breaking news story, have always worked with those on the ground to secure a story but the change in media business models and security worries mean fixers have increasingly taken on the role of journalists, with the lines becoming blurred (Plaut & Klein, 2019: 1698). The 2003 US-led invasion of Iraq and subsequent civil war is widely seen as a turning point after which fixers not only were used to help facilitate news gathering but have also been used to uncover and report the story, even carrying out interviews if it is safer for them to do so (Murrell, 2010: 133). The crisis in Afghanistan following the rapid and unexpected return of Taliban rule immediately exposed the international media's reliance on local journalists and fixers. In the wake of the collapse of the Afghan government, UK media companies wrote an open letter to Prime Minister Boris Johnson appealing to the UK government to expand its visa programme to Afghans who have worked for them over the past 20 years. The US media had made a similar appeal a few weeks earlier. The UK news organisations stated in their letter (*The Guardian*, 2021):

> If left behind, those Afghan journalists and media employees who have played such a vital role informing the British public by working for British media will be left at the risk of persecution, of physical harm, incarceration, torture, or death.

What does the incorporation of user-generated content and material from local journalists or fixers mean for the way news agencies frame a story and their traditional role as gatekeepers? Academic literature on gatekeeping dates back to the 1950s, making it one of the oldest social science concepts adapted for the study of journalism. It began with David Manning White's investigation of a wire editor from a regional newspaper and his reasons for the selection of stories which he chose to use. The conclusion was that the selection was highly subjective and based on the gatekeeper's own experiences and attitudes (White, 1950: 390). That conclusion has been widely disputed in numerous subsequent studies and led to attempts to conceptualise and categorise news values (e.g. Galtung & Ruge, 1965, and subsequent refinements such as Harcup & O'Neill, 2017). But the current disintermediation of traditional news organisations through social media has prompted a radical rethink of such theories. As Amazeen states (2020: 96):

> Whereas elite gatekeepers once largely determined the quantity and quality of mediated content, the distributed network model of present-day media enables anyone with a keyboard and an Internet connection to create and share their own content. Consequently, along with this democratization of content has come a tidal wave of misinformation.

One of those new concepts has been labelled "gatewatching" in which websites or social media platforms are "curated" and contain information or links from diverse sources, some of which might cater to minority audience interests (unconstrained by the limited time/space and the need to cater for a targeted audience that characterise, for example, traditional broadcast journalism) (Bruns, 2003: 33). The concept is "less like that of the traditional journalist than it is like that of the specialist librarian who constantly surveys the information becoming available in a variety of media and serves as a guide to the most relevant sources when approached by information-seekers" (ibid: 34). Gatewatchers fundamentally publicise news (by pointing to sources) rather than publish it (by compiling an apparently complete report from the available sources) (ibid).

Not surprisingly, news agencies argue that far from being outdated, gatekeeping is more valuable than ever since they are ideally placed given their long tradition of news editing and production desks to distinguish between important information circulating on social media, which might complement their own stories, and fake news, rumour and conspiracy theories. Arguably, the mechanics of gatekeeping (not the concept) have subtly changed since the news agency correspondent in the field may no longer be the first to witness news. But the agency

Back to the future 71

may well still be the first to verify its accuracy. AFP's Chetwynd explains the shift and where he sees the value of a news agency:

> We are in a sense no longer the gatekeepers, but what we can bring is this incredibly powerful on-the-ground verification of things that move very fast. We are less at the start of the information chain, because every whisper and rumour is already flying around, but the value we can bring by being on the ground and using the network is incredibly powerful.

In performing this role, the agencies are effectively colonising third-party material, absorbing it into their own news "container" and validating its value and authenticity. This requires a well-tuned fact-checking infrastructure since once material is incorporated into an agency's own news feed or platform, the likely assumption from the audience will be that the agency is responsible for it.

The issue becomes particularly sensitive when working with fixers, freelancers or stringers who are reporting back from crisis areas where the news agency might not today have its own staff. If working for an agency, these local sources know they need to play by the agency's rules of objectivity and impartiality. But their work will inevitably, if only unconsciously, contribute to the framing of a story. The fact that fixers, for example, are able to go through their list of local contacts and offer a selection of sources to a correspondent, or file material based on that selection themselves, inherently influences editorial content (Plaut & Klein, 2019: 1708). It is essential, therefore, that the agency editing desk recognises the fixer's "editorial agency" and is transparent about it. In the long-running Syrian conflict, where Western correspondents have been under consistent threat, the reliance on local reporting has become steadily greater and prompted the agencies to place increased emphasis on training local staff. AFP's Chetwynd said the agency had taken enormous efforts to tell the story of the Syrian civil war from both sides. On the one side of the conflict, AFP had maintained access to the Assad government in Damascus, while on the other side, it had set up a bureau on the Turkish border, cycling into Syria its own correspondents, building contacts and training local journalists. Training sessions were held in Turkey and online, creating over time a trusted network that could shoot still pictures, gather video material or just provide information.

> "We put the bar extremely high on using (social media) material," Chetwynd said. "There were times when images were clearly

significant and we used them. But we put the bar very, very high on the basis that it if we put the AFP stamp on that, it is no use having a disclaimer sourcing it to somebody else..."

Reuters ran its operations from its Beirut bureau, with reporters talking regularly with sources inside Syria, complemented by the occasional trip inside the country. Like the other agencies, it made use of user-generated content as long as it could be verified.

It would, of course, be easy for news agencies to incorporate user-generated content into their reporting and include a disclaimer saying the material came from elsewhere. But clients' expectation is that the material has been verified, especially at a time when news agencies are spotlighting their verification expertise. Inevitably, in such a polarised conflict where information has been weaponised, media organisations have been sucked into controversy. Most notably, a heated debate has arisen around the Syrian Civil Defence Force, widely known as the White Helmets. According to *The Guardian* newspaper, the rescue workers, who operate in rebel-held areas attacked by the Syrian regime of President Bashar al-Assad, have been a target of a disinformation campaign supported by the Russian government (which provides military support to Assad) (2017). In such instances, the agencies have once again fallen back on tried and tested norms of attempting to tell a story from multiple perspectives and being transparent about sourcing.

The danger within

The risks to the reputation and credibility of the news agencies in an era of social media do not come solely from outside their own walls. The agencies all updated guidelines *for their own journalists* about ten years ago to take into account the ubiquitous nature of social media, treading a fine line between embracing the benefits and warning of potential pitfalls.

In a media environment in which audiences expect to see the human side of the journalist behind a story and hear his or her views about it, the agencies are all too aware that it requires just one tweet to be sucked into controversy. Journalists are increasingly expected to brand themselves and promote their work and news organisation (Molyneux, 2015; Molyneux & Holton, 2015; Molyneux, Holton, & Lewis, 2018) and those working for news agencies are subject to the same pressure, particularly in respect of Twitter. The platform has become one of the most important communication vehicles in the field of journalism, with more than 200 million active users worldwide. In fact, it has taken on the character of a convenient, cheap and effective "beat" for journalists, offering a large range of sources who would otherwise be hard to approach (Broersma & Graham, 2013: 447). Such networking tools are essential in an environment in which news gathering resources have often been cut and in which reporters are expected to write more stories (ibid). But it is a platform that also contains numerous potential traps for agency journalists as the nature of the business embraces retail audiences as well as traditional wholesale clients. As Griessner observes (2012: 7):

> While most of the news media communicate with the public, news agencies are based on communicating with media clients. But as the wire services expand onto social media platforms, they also enter the realm of direct communication to the public …

One of the main drivers as news agencies seek to broaden their market through retail offerings online and widen distribution channels is profile and brand awareness. But to do that within the constraints of the news agency straitjacket of objectivity and impartiality – and without sparking public controversy – is a delicate balancing act. Typical of the guidelines to agency journalists are those issued by AP which states:[9]

> AP journalists are encouraged to maintain accounts on social networks, and must identify themselves in their profiles as being with AP if they use the accounts for work in any way … Staffers are encouraged to share AP content in all formats to social platforms.

AP journalists are told to avoid expressions of opinion on contentious issues and to be particularly wary of "re-tweeting" information, ensuring that language is added to make sure it is the opinion of someone else. Indeed, in May 2021, AP fired a reporter in its Western US Phoenix bureau, for violating its social media policy. AP would not say what the reporter, Emily Wilder, had written but news reports have focused on what appears to have been pro-Palestinian tweets.[10] The sacking provoked a backlash within AP, with 100 journalists signing a letter expressing concern over how she was treated and the editorial management team launching a review of its policies. The AP's story about the incident written by journalist David Bauder included the telling remark that the incident "illustrates how it can be difficult for a news organisation, particularly a traditionalist like The Associated Press, to handle the free-wheeling nature of social media" (2021).

This controversy aside, when following politicians on social media accounts, AP journalists are urged to connect with those on both sides of a given issue or campaign. Contrary to many daily newspapers with comprehensive online operations, AP does not operate an "online first" policy, stating that its journalists should not share urgent breaking news they have confirmed over social media accounts until they have provided it to the appropriate desk, adding "exclusive material and important tips should not be shared online before the related story has been published." Reuters guidelines, discussed below, also clearly state: "do not scoop the wire."

In fact, the Reuters guidelines[11] read almost as a carbon copy:

> We want to encourage you to use social media approaches in your journalism but we also need to make sure that you are fully aware of the risks – especially those that threaten our hard-earned reputation for independence and freedom from bias or our brand.
>
> Whether we think it is fair or not, other media will use your social media output as Reuters comment on topical stories. And we will play into the hands of our critics unless we take care:
>
> - Resist the temptation to respond in anger to those you regard as mistaken or ill-tempered;
> - Think about how you'd feel if your content was cited on the front page of a leading newspaper or website or blog as Reuters comment on an issue;
> - Don't suspend your critical faculties. It's simple to share a link on Twitter, Facebook and other networks but as a Reuters journalist if you repeat something that turns out to be a hoax, or suggests you support a particular line of argument, then you risk undermining your own credibility and that of Reuters News.

The Reuters social media guidelines also make an important point about how the professional and private persona of a journalist have become intertwined and blurred but recommend that its journalists try to keep separate social media accounts. Reuters warns that everyone leaves an online footprint and a determined critic can soon build up a picture of political preferences and affiliations which might create a perception of bias. AFP also encourages its journalists to open social media accounts while issuing the same cautionary sentiments, not least, it says, because AFP journalists are interacting directly with the public without the second pair of eyes and the traditional safety net provided by an editing desk. AFP urges journalists to use a disclaimer on their social media accounts, employing a form of words which has become familiar on Twitter such as "the views expressed here are my own. Links and re-tweets are not endorsements." It also adds a clear statement about the value it sees in a social media presence in that it adds visibility to its journalism, saying (AFP press release 2013):

> The presence of AFP journalists on social networks helps build the agency's credibility across the Internet and shows that AFP has a solid presence across the spectrum of digital and traditional media.

When it comes to Bloomberg, the agency also sees social media as an excellent vehicle for promoting its work but, in unison with its rivals, warns against expressing political opinions or advocacy and says posts should never express bias based on race, sex, religion or nationality.

However, the most comprehensive guidelines do not mean that things cannot go wrong and there have been high-profile incidents that have threatened reputations. In 2006, Reuters was forced to withdraw 920 pictures by one of its freelance photographers after it was alleged that he had digitally altered two images taken in Lebanon. Bloggers spotted that smoke on one of Adnan Hajj's pictures appeared to have been made darker than it actually was, while flares had been added to an image of an Israeli jet. Reuters global picture editor at the time Tom Szlukovenyi said the manipulation undermined trust in Hajj's entire body of work, adding that could be no graver breach of Reuters standards for the agency's photographers than the deliberate manipulation of an image. Hajj denied deliberate manipulation of the material. As a result of the affair, new Reuters guidelines set strict technical limits on the use of Photoshop software.

In addition, all the agencies have become alert to constant cyber-attacks, both Reuters and the AP falling victim to false tweets after their official agency accounts were hacked. These have focused on the Syrian conflict that has become fertile ground for false information as mainstream news organisations draw on local sources of information and as cyber-warfare becomes more prevalent. In 2013, AP's Twitter feed was hacked, with one false post stating: *"Breaking: Two Explosions in the White House and Barack Obama is injured."* Not surprisingly, US financial markets were unsettled, with the Dow Jones index falling around 150 points as the message was re-tweeted. An investigation revealed that the attack was probably carried out by a group of computer hackers claiming to support Syrian President Bashar al-Assad called the Syrian Electronic Army. It has claimed to have been behind similar attacks on the social media feeds of, among others, AFP, the BBC, Sky News Arabia, Al Jazeera and CBS News. In another incident, the main Reuters.com website was hacked and a faked interview purporting to be with a Syrian rebel leader was posted on a journalist's blog. In addition, 22 false tweets were sent under the Reuters name, some of them containing false reports of rebel losses incurred in fighting with Syrian government forces. *The Christian Science Monitor* reported (2012):

> The Syrian civil war, with limited access for journalists but a proliferation of rebels and regime supporters with smart phones and Internet connections, has been a particularly fertile propaganda battlefield. Far too often, unconfirmed claims emerging on Twitter or YouTube are taken as fact, and presumably the pro-Assad hackers were seeking to amplify this phenomenon in recent days.
>
> What good does it do them? It's hard to imagine much. These kinds of hoaxes are run to the ground fairly quickly and the only people they appear to take in are those inclined to want to believe them in the first place. But they're certainly a reminder of the need for caution in approaching online information. If something looks extraordinary, assume it is until you have solid confirmation otherwise.

Covering Trump

The hacking incidents were a salutary reminder of the dangers attached to social media and high profile, polarised international conflicts such as that in Syria. But the news agencies have also faced a serious challenge as they themselves have been repeatedly labelled "fake news" as they conduct routine cover of day-to-day political news, not least the Trump presidency.

Trump made criticising the media into a daily occurrence, with some counts reckoning that he labelled them as fake news more than 2,000 times during his time in office. He declared in a tweet in February 2017 (*The Washington Post*): "FAKE NEWS media is the enemy of the American people," citing the *New York Times*, CNN, NBC, ABC and CBS. The agencies didn't escape Trump's wrath. He lashed out against AP in 2018, tweeting: "AP headline was very different from my quote and meaning in the story. They just can't help themselves. FAKE NEWS!" But in the daily sparring with journalists, there were also unexpected turns. Once, when the veteran Reuters White House reporter Steve Holland stood up to ask a question, Trump called him "a high-quality person," adding, "Now he'll probably hit me with a bad one" (cited in the *New York Times*, 2018). But Holland's White House reporter colleague, Jeff Mason, was berated by Trump for being "rude" in an angry exchange just a few months later and had a number of run-ins with the president when questions became uncomfortable.

Despite provocation, the agencies stuck to the tried and tested recipe of fact-based reporting. Typical of this response was a memo sent to Reuters staff by then editor-in-chief Stephen Adler just 12 days into the Trump presidency, 12 days he said had been "especially challenging for us in the news business (The Baron, 2017).[12] Adler laid out a message of "business as usual" by reporting fairly and honestly and remaining impartial. He said in the memo:

> It's not every day that a US president calls journalist "among the most dishonest human beings on earth" or that his chief strategist dubs the media "the opposition party." It's hardly surprising that the air is thick with questions and theories about how to cover the new Administration.
>
> So, what is the Reuters answer? To oppose the administration? To appease it? To boycott its briefings? To use our platform to rally support for the media? All these ideas are out there, and they may be right for some news operations, but they don't make sense for Reuters. We already know what to do because we do it every day, and we do it all over the world.

Adler told his journalists never to be intimidated and gave them practical guidance, adhering to the Reuters Trust principles[13] and operating with calm integrity. Asked about how this worked in practice, White House reporter Mason said (The Baron, 2021):

> One thing that I hope distinguished my own questioning was remaining (true) to what the core of Reuters is – that sense of neutrality, that sense of just asking a question neutrally, writing neutrally, staying straight down the middle, (which) you can do, and should do regardless of who is in office in the White House, regardless of the rhetoric that comes out of his or her mouth.

The other major agencies took a similar line, emphasising their adherence to facts. In the wake of Trump's 2020 election defeat, which he refused to accept, AP cited its "robust factual reporting" as the president challenged the integrity of the results (AP Annual Report, 2020).

AFP spoke of the importance of fact-checking as disinformation and conspiracy theories "literally exploded" after the November 7 election (Rouach, 2020), while Bloomberg News ran into controversy as Trump withdrew the agency's credentials ahead of the 2020 campaign.[14] Bloomberg News quoted its editor-in-chief John Micklethwait as saying that the accusation of bias couldn't be further from the truth. "We have covered Donald Trump fairly and in an unbiased way since he became a candidate in 2015 and will continue to do so despite the restrictions imposed by the Trump campaign," Micklethwait said.

Conclusion

Whether they like it or not, the news agencies have been catapulted into the world of social media. What began as a tense and uneasy relationship in the early 2000s has since settled into one in which the benefits are being harvested and where the dangers have been clearly identified (although not always contained).

Like other news outlets, the agencies have embraced social media tools to aid the production and distribution of news, build networks of sources and incorporate user-generated content into their reporting that might otherwise never have been seen in the analogue era. The coverage of breaking news stories (their bread and butter since the 19th century), whether it be a terror attack close to their main newsroom in a Western capital or conflict in far-away places, has been transformed by the ability to monitor, verify and use mobile phone footage and eyewitness accounts from people caught up in events. In fact, when it comes to covering the conflict in countries such as Syria, the dangers posed to Western journalists have left the news agencies little choice but to rely on third-party material which by the very nature of the conflict could be partisan. And the chaotic days following the Taliban's seizure of power in Afghanistan graphically illustrated just how dependent they, and other Western media outlets, are on fixers, translators and local journalists. This does not, however, mean that the agencies have ceded control of the news file. On the contrary, they have kept a firm grip of their role as *de facto* gatekeepers of the news even if there are cases where the role changes subtly from eyewitness reporting to the verification of user-generated content. The hesitancy to link to third-party material that might, for example, be more typical of opinion-based journalism means that links in stories posted on their consumer facing news sites tend to be to their own content or to third-party content that has been carefully verified and incorporated into the news file. As a result, readers are often kept within the container of an apnews.com or reuters.com site rather than being directed to outside sources. External links embedded in stories might typically be to underlying press releases, reports or comments made on Twitter but tend to be more limited when compared to the online sites of some major popular newspapers or broadcasters.

The agencies have also clearly identified and seized the opportunity to build on their long history of plain vanilla, fact-based journalism to underscore their hard news credentials in the face of the tidal wave of disinformation, fake news and conspiracy theories. As such, they are exploiting a recent backlash against social media as consumers show signs of a growing appreciation of fact-based news where they are left to make up their own mind about events. As the former editor-in-chief of Reuters Mark Wood said:

> I always thought ... that the demand for reliable, trustworthy news would grow, having sort of disappeared in the forest of "it's all on social media isn't it," that now there is so much manipulation that the demand for news and facts you can trust is bound to increase and that's a pretty good place to be.

Typical of a culture that has at times been cautious in adopting new technologies, the agencies have issued clear guidelines to their journalists about the dangers of social media and the speed with which, for example, tweets and re-tweets can endanger their long-standing reputation for impartiality and freedom from bias. In doing so, the news agencies have sought to remain above the fray as mainstream media in countries, such as the United States and Britain, become increasingly polarised and partisan in their coverage. Inevitably, the news agencies have at times been sucked into controversy, particularly during the Trump presidency and when covering volatile developments in the long-running Syrian civil war. But compared with the divisive and at times vitriolic public arguments played out on social media about the news operations of, for example, Fox News, the *New York Times* or CNN, the agencies have managed to remain largely inconspicuous in the background. The question posed in the context of US politics is whether this approach of studious neutrality actually played into Trump's hands. In the opinion of the Columbia Journalism Review, the former president "ruthlessly gamed old-school journalists' commitment to covering both sides of the story, winning more than equal time for his lies..." (2020). That evaluation of news coverage during the Trump presidency did not focus on the news agencies, analysing instead mainstream US print and broadcast media and asking whether impartiality in the face of such events was morally inadequate and let Trump "off the hook." The same question could certainly be asked of the news agencies and their coverage of Trump, but it is difficult to see what else they could have done. In the final analysis, they dug in, sticking to their policy of verifying information, calling out false information, and trying to uphold their commitment to impartiality.

Notes

1. See Chapter 2, p. 55.
2. Research for the 2021 Digital News Report was conducted by YouGov (and their partners) using an online questionnaire at the end of January/beginning of February 2021. Audiences were sampled in 46 markets.
3. Barrett was speaking in July 2021 at a British Council-sponsored conference for journalism students called Future News Worldwide.
4. Through this Facebook is to provide funding to the Reuters fact-checking unit in exchange for assessments of the authenticity of content on its Facebook and Instagram platforms. See: https://www.reuters.com/article/rpb-facebookuk-idUKKBN21C14M
5. Author's italics.
6. The Poynter Institute was founded in 1975 and is a non-profit journalism school and research organisation in St. Petersburg, Florida. The school is the owner of the Tampa Bay Times newspaper.
7. See: https://www.poynter.org/ifcn-fact-checkers-code-of-principles/
8. Gatekeeping can be defined as "the process of selecting, writing, editing, positioning, scheduling, repeating and otherwise massaging information to become news" (Shoemaker, Vos & Reese, 2009).
9. AP – The Social Networks, available from: https://www.google.com/url?sa=t&rct=j&q=&esrc=s&source=web&cd=&ved=2ahUKEwjuqr7N6LXyAhUzgv0HHSF6BTAQFnoECAMQAQ&url=https%3A%2F%2Fwww.ap.org%2Fassets%2Fdocuments%2Fsocial_media_06022021.pdf&usg=AOvVaw2ZzD0s7uZpMlphQkgUPK5l
10. For a summary of the controversy, see: https://www.poynter.org/newsletters/2021/the-associated-press-fired-a-reporter-over-social-media-use-and-what-it-means-for-other-news-outlets/?__cf_chl_jschl_tk__=pmd_ZDRpbyVhFse.Wpj9ZezDth87KBTBZyd1oWIrNeKkN5A-1630008376-0-gqNtZGzNAmWjcnBszQa9
11. The version published in 2010 is referred to here. Material is also incorporated into a series of webpages entitled Standards and Values. See: https://www.reutersagency.com/en/about/standards-values/#Social_media_guidelines
12. The Baron is a website that forms a discussion forum for current and past Reuters employees (predominantly from the journalism side of the house but also business). It includes news, gossip and commentary about the news agency.
13. See Chapter 1, p. 23.
14. The move was in reaction to the agency's refusal to investigate its owner Michael Bloomberg who was running as a Democratic presidential candidate in primaries.

References

Agence France-Presse. 2020. Annual report. https://view.afp.com/2020-annual-report/home-page/p/1

Agence France-Presse Press Release. 2013. AFP updates guidelines on using social media. https://www.afp.com/en/agency/press-releases-newsletter/afp-updates-guidelines-using-social-media

Agence France-Presse Press Release. 2020. AFP consolidates its place as global fact check leader with new German service. https://www.afp.com/en/agency/press-releases-newsletter/afp-consolidates-its-place-global-fact-check-leader-new-german-service

Allan, S., 2014. Witnessing in crisis: Photo-reportage of terror attacks in Boston and London. *Media, War & Conflict*, 7(2), pp. 133–151.

Amazeen, M.A., 2020. Journalistic interventions: The structural factors affecting the global emergence of fact-checking. *Journalism*, 21(1), pp. 95–111.

Associated Press. 2020. Annual report. https://www.ap.org/about/annual-report/

Bakir, V. and McStay, A., 2018. Fake news and the economy of emotions: Problems, causes, solutions. *Digital Journalism*, 6(2), pp. 154–175.

Bauder, D., 2021. AP says it is reviewing social media policies after firing. *AP*, 25 May 2021. https://apnews.com/article/social-media-media-business-arts-and-entertainment-55cee73bd1da80790ad4aacf3cb2e339

Belair-Gagnon, V., 2015. *Social media at BBC news: The remaking of crisis reporting*. New York: Routledge.

Boaden, H., 2008. The role of citizen journalism in modern democracy. *The BBC* (online), 13 November 2008. http://www.bbc.co.uk/blogs/legacy/theeditors/2008/11/the_role_of_citizen_journalism.html

Broersma, M. and Graham, T., 2013. Twitter as a news source. How Dutch and British newspapers used tweets in their news coverage, 2007–2011. *Journalism Practice*, 7(4), pp. 446–464.

Bruns, A., 2003. Gatewatching not gatekeeping: Collaborative online news. *Media International Australia Incorporating Culture and Policy: Quarterly Journal of Media Research and Resources*, 107, pp. 31–44.

Columbia Journalism Review, 2020. How the press covered the last four years of Trump. https://www.cjr.org/special_report/coverage-trump-presidency-2020-election.php

Deuze, M., 2005. What is journalism? Professional identity and ideology of journalists reconsidered. *Journalism*, 6(4), pp. 442–464.

Eyewitness Media Hub, 2015. *Making secondary trauma a primary issue: A study of eyewitness media and vicarious trauma on the digital frontline.* http://eyewitnessmediahub.com/research/vicarious-trauma

Galtung, J. and Ruge, M.H., 1965. The structure of foreign news: The presentation of the Congo, Cuba and Cyprus crises in four Norwegian newspapers. *Journal of Peace Research*, 2(1), pp. 64–90.

Graves, L. and Cherubini, F., 2016. *The rise of fact-checking sites in Europe.* Oxford: Reuters Institute for the Study of Journalism.

Griessner, M.C., 2012. *News agencies and social media*. Oxford: Reuters Institute for the Study of Journalism.

Harcup, T. and O'Neill, D., 2017. What is news? Galtung and Ruge revisited (again). *Journalism Studies*, 18(12), pp. 1470–1488.

Jukes, S., 2020. *Journalism and emotion*. London: Sage.

Molyneux, L., 2015. What journalists retweet: Opinion, humor, and brand development on Twitter. *Journalism*, 16(7), pp. 920–935.

Molyneux, L. and Holton, A.E., 2015. Branding (health) journalism: Perceptions, practices, and emerging norms. *Digital Journalism*, 3(2), pp. 225–242.

Molyneux, L., Holton, A.E. and Lewis, S.C., 2018. How journalists engage in branding on twitter: Individual, organizational, and institutional levels. *Information, Communication & Society*, 21(10), pp. 1386–1401.

Murrell, C., 2010. Baghdad Bureaux: An exploration of the interconnected world of fixers and correspondents at the BBC and CNN. *Media, War & Conflict*, 3(2), pp. 125–137.

Newman, N., Fletcher, R., Schulz, A., Andi, S., Robertson, C.T. and Nielsen, R.K., 2021. Reuters institute digital news report 2021. *Reuters Institute for the Study of Journalism*.

New York Times. 2018. I could be doing this all day. Trump delights in sparring with the press. *New York Times*, 26 September 2018. https://www.nytimes.com/2018/09/26/business/media/trump-news-conference-media.html

Ofcom. 2018. Scrolling news: The changing face of online news consumption. www.ofcom.org.uk/__data/assets/pdf_file/0022/115915/Scrolling-News.pdf

Plaut, S. and Klein, P., 2019. "Fixing" the journalist-fixer relationship: A critical look towards developing Best practices in global reporting. *Journalism Studies*, 20(12), pp. 1696–1713.

Reuters, 2021a. Reuters expands efforts to combat misinformation with extension of fact-checking partnership with Facebook in the United Kingdom. https://www.reuters.com/article/rpb-facebookuk-idUKKBN21C14M

Reuters, 2021b. About Reuters fact check. https://www.reuters.com/fact-check/about

Rouach, H., 2020. Briefing on US presidential election. In *Agence France-Presse Annual Report*. https://view.afp.com/2020-annual-report/home-page/p/1

Sambrook, R., 2010. *Are foreign correspondents redundant? The changing face of international news*. Oxford: Reuters Institute for the Study of Journalism.

Shoemaker, P.J., Vos, T.P. and Reese, S.D., 2009. Journalists as gatekeepers. In *The handbook of journalism studies* (pp. 93–107). New York: Routledge.

Singer, J., 2015. Out of bounds—Professional norms as boundary markers. In Carlson, M. & Lewis, C. (Eds.) *Boundaries of journalism: Professionalism, practices and participation*. London: Routledge.

The Baron, 2017. Covering Trump the Reuters way. *The Baron*, 1 February 2017. https://www.thebaron.info/news/article/2017/02/01/covering-trump-the-reuters-way

The Baron, 2021. Jeff Mason. *The Baron*, 8 April 2021. https://thebaron.info/the-barons-briefings/jeff-mason

The Christian Science Monitor, 2012. Reuters hacked by pro Assad propagandists again, this time on Twitter. *The Christian Science Monitor*, 5 August 2012. https://www.csmonitor.com/World/Security-Watch/Backchannels/2012/0805/Reuters-hacked-by-pro-Assad-propagandists-again-this-time-on-Twitter

The Guardian, 2017. How Syria's White Helmets became victims of an online propaganda machine. *The Guardian*, 18 December 2017. https://www.theguardian.com/world/2017/dec/18/syria-white-helmets-conspiracy-theories

The Guardian, 2021. Open letter warns of brutal Taliban reprisals against Afghan reporters. *The Guardian*, 4 August 2012. https://www.theguardian.com/world/2021/aug/04/open-letter-warns-of-brutal-taliban-reprisals-against-afghan-reporters

The Washington Post, 2017. Trump calls the media the enemy of the American People. *The Washington Post*, 17 February 2017. https://www.washingtonpost.com/news/post-politics/wp/2017/02/17/trump-calls-the-media-the-enemy-of-the-american-people/

Waterson, J., 2021. How GB News is bringing US-style opinionated TV news to the UK. *The Guardian*, 12 June 2021. https://www.theguardian.com/media/2021/jun/12/gb-news-bringing-us-style-opinionated-tv-news-uk

White, D.M., 1950. The "Gate Keeper": A case study in the selection of news. *Journalism Quarterly*, 27(4), pp. 383–390.

Williams, A., Wahl-Jorgensen, K. and Wardle, C., 2011. More real and less packaged: Audience discourses on amateur news content and their effects on journalism practice. In Anden-Papadopoulos, K. & Pantti, M. (Eds.) *Amateur images and global news*. Chicago: Intellect, University of Chicago Press.

Zelizer, B., 2000. Foreword. In Sparks, C. & Tulloch, J. (Eds.) *Tabloid tales—Global debates over media standards*. Oxford: Rowman & Littlefield.

4 Collaboration, community and state actors

> We look beyond the short-term news agenda, and the need to generate clicks. Instead we take time to dig deep, led by the facts not by political or corporate agendas. We do not cower from difficult stories and we seek to listen to voices that are often overlooked ... We believe people are stronger when they work together. We take a collective approach to how we tackle problems, share skills and enable change.
>
> The Bureau of Investigative Journalism

Introduction

News agencies live on scoops and hard-breaking news, whether it be pivotal moments in history such as the fall of the Berlin Wall or a central banker's market-moving pronouncements on an arcane aspect of monetary policy. Their reputation for being able to deliver fast and accurate news has been built on a seamless network of foreign correspondents, local journalists and fixers on the ground as eyewitnesses to unfolding stories, coupled with blanket coverage of diarised news conferences and a growing capacity to monitor and verify material emanating from social media feeds.

But are there alternative ways of covering the news that might challenge the agencies' predominantly Western view of the world? Might other methods, including a more activist or more collective approach as espoused by the Bureau of Investigative Journalism, actually be necessary in today's digital news environment? And might the news agencies be tempted to move into long-form journalism in an attempt to diversify their offering into in-depth investigative reporting?

The emergence of collaborative news networks, including, for example, those pulled together to sift through the enormous data leaks that made up what have become known as the "Panama Papers," "Paradise Papers" and "Pandora Papers" in, respectively, 2016, 2017 and 2021

DOI: 10.4324/9781003029656-5

runs counter to the natural instinct of the agencies to scoop the opposition, tightly guard their sources and maintain control of the news agenda. Organisations such as the US-based non-profit International Consortium of Investigative Journalists (ICIJ) and the London-based Bureau of Investigative Journalism have built global networks of journalists to work on complex investigative stories and share their results. It is a collective – and alternative – approach to journalism that can take months to yield results and pools resources. At the same time, a series of collaborations such as the Dutch non-profit *Global Voices* is emerging to practise a form of community and participatory journalism designed to counter the dominant narrative of news produced by mainstream Western outlets. In addition, the past few years have witnessed the rapid expansion of what might be called "state actors" seeking to exert soft power through their media output. State-funded or government-backed news operations, such as China's CGTN[1] and Russia's RT,[2] have invested millions building news hubs in major centres, such as London and Washington DC, in their attempt to put across their alternative, non-Western view of the news agenda despite deep suspicion from Western governments and regulators that they are simply peddling state propaganda.

This chapter focuses on the emergence of such new players on the scene – collaborative news networks, the rise of a globally-coordinated community-oriented journalism that promotes an empathic form of reporting and the growing presence of state actors. It explores whether their proliferation is finally changing the model of reporting foreign news from faraway places and whether this, in turn, might challenge the hegemonic dominance of the news agencies and other influential mainstream Western news outlets with a global influence, such as the BBC and CNN. In his theoretical discussion of news models, Peter Berglez argues that a truly global journalism has a distinct epistemology that yields *different* interpretations of the world. He states (2008: 247):

> The national outlook puts the nation-state at the centre of things when framing social reality, while the global outlook instead seeks to understand and explain how economic, political, social and ecological practices, processes and problems in different parts of the world affect each other, are interlocked, or share commonalities.

The question is whether the "counter hegemonic" networks (Painter, 2008) that are now emerging can succeed in challenging the view of the world presented through the ubiquitous flow of stories, news photographs and, above all, video footage generated by the major news agencies.

Taking a different approach

The rise of the three main agencies in the 19th century, documented in detail in Chapter 1, had two main unforeseen consequences. Firstly, their development was key to the emergence of what became the Anglo-American objectivity paradigm, fact-based reporting and the "inverted pyramid" story construction, seen as one of the hallmarks of objectivity (Porwancher, 2011: 191). Far from abandoning these values and practices in the face of social media and the demands for a more partisan approach, the agencies have held their ground and actively sought to promote impartiality and fact-based journalism as a badge of honour. Secondly, the agencies' historic roots and ties to the major colonial powers of that era – Britain, France and Germany – created a lasting legacy that, it is argued, can be still detected today. Far from being limited to the United States and the United Kingdom, the values implicit in the agencies' news culture spread as a result of colonial power well beyond their borders. As Williams observes (2011: 46):

> Colonialism not only moulded how international news is gathered, processed and disseminated today, but also had a profound impact on audience expectations of what international news should be.

While the news agencies' comfortable alliance collapsed in the face of opposition and the growth of radio in the 1930s, the previous chapters have illustrated how they have to this day remained a homogenous group in terms of their common adherence to similar news values and fact-based journalism. They have tried to maintain a firm grip on the global hard news agenda, particularly in supplying video footage to the major broadcasters, and resisted trends that might undermine their role as gatekeepers during successive waves of media transformation, disruption and the proliferation of social media content.

The 1980s ushered in 24-hour rolling broadcast news channels, all of which followed and perpetuated the same news gathering, production and distribution channels as their predecessors, namely, a standard model of Anglo-American journalism. CNN was launched in 1980 and today claims that its global arm, CNN International, reaches

370 million household and hotel rooms worldwide.[3] Shortly after its launch, other major Western nations followed suit, with an explosion of 24/7 satellite news channels around the globe (Rai & Cottle, 2007: 51). The BBC set up BBC World Service Television in 1991, later changing its name and branding to today's BBC World News. Although radically different in their editorial approach, and ushering a far more opinionated form of journalism, by 1996 both Fox News and MSNBC had launched their 24-hour news services in the United States to rival CNN. Despite their introduction of partisan views and an element of "shock jock" journalism inherited from talk radio, these newly launched news outlets had one thing in common – their view of international news was from a Western perspective and was rooted in the Anglo-American tradition of journalism pioneered by the news agencies more than a century earlier. It was frustration at this, and charges of cultural imperialism, which were partly responsible for the emergence of another wave of new stations whose goal was, at least on the face of it, to challenge this world view. This has included, amongst more than 100 newcomers, prominent names, such as al-Jazeera (founded in 1996) and al-Arabiya (2003) in the Arab world, Euronews (1993), China's 24-hour-news English language channel as part of the CCTV network (2000), Russia Today (2005), France 24 (2006) and Iran's Press TV (2007).

Whether this revolution in broadcasting has done anything to counter the dominance of the Western news agenda (sometimes referred to as "the West to the rest"), is a matter of academic debate. Thussu has argued that despite a certain democratisation of news flows little actually changed and the major players remained Western (2003: 119). The rise of transnational media conglomerates such as News Corporation led by Rupert Murdoch and the continued power of Reuters Television and APTN with their screen-ready bulletins that can be slotted seamlessly into a client's news programming only reinforced this (2003: 120). For Thussu and others, the charges of cultural imperialism in UNESCO's 1980 report of a neo-colonial approach to global news were still valid.[4] A counterargument maintains that the rise in global satellite channels has resulted in a new form of international reporting that has gone beyond narrow national interests and sets aside traditional Western news framing hierarchies (Volkmer, 1999; 2003). A prime example of this, it is argued, came during the US-led invasion of Iraq in 2003 when the presence of Arabic broadcasters and their focus on civilian victims of the war provided an alternative narrative to sanitised images of Western missiles being fired by coalition forces.

The advent of social media that followed has, of course, brought about far more sweeping changes than the introduction of 24-hour rolling news channels and the democratising impact on the practice of journalism has been well documented (e.g. Allan, 2013; Bruns, 2003, 2011). As previous chapters have illustrated, the news agencies have embraced social media as a reporting, networking and distribution tool and sought to guard against potential pitfalls. In a social media world, individuals who sometimes find themselves thrust into the role of reporter as an eyewitness to a crime, disaster or various crises can exert their presence *outside, through* and *within* mainstream media (Cottle, 2009: xi). But much of the material does not see the light of day and in the past decade, a number of non-profit organisations have attempted to harness this diversity of content to build new global networks that bear an uncanny resemblance to an international news agency (albeit on a far smaller scale than the corporately-organised likes of Reuters, AP and AFP). Often, these organisations draw on a core team of established journalists but their goals are subtly different – sometimes they specialise in performing investigative tasks that might once have been considered to be outside the capability of mainstream news organisations; sometimes their goal is to collate and connect marginalised voices which might otherwise not be heard in a Western-centric reporting operation; sometimes, they involve a form of activism that stops just short of advocacy or campaigning. In many of the cases, they champion an empathic form of journalism that aims to promote a better understanding of local issues. The next sections of this chapter explore such initiatives, the model of collaborative journalism and a community-based approach to news.

Breaking the taboo about collaboration

Collaboration in the news world is far from a recent phenomenon and, ironically, it was the news agencies that pioneered such approaches. The Associated Press came into being in 1846 specifically because US newspapers could not afford to cover the Mexican-American war (Lewis, 2018: 5). Five newspapers pooled their resources and sent a reporter to Mexico who sent his dispatches back. Later, the European agencies Reuters, Havas and Wolff would effectively carve up the world between themselves in their news alliance, agreeing on the free exchange of news within their cartel.[5] Today, at times of war (e.g. the invasions of Iraq in 1991 and 2003) and routinely for major political events, the agencies and other news organisations have agreed to a reporting "pool" when space for multiple reporting teams is limited (or in conflict zones where the risks might be high).

By a similar token, foreign correspondents operating in a tight community in the field often collaborate and seek out each other's company. But at the same time, there is a deep-seated instinct not to collaborate and a desire to scoop the opposition. The legendary American foreign correspondent Martha Gellhorn begins her 1940 novel *A Stricken Field* by depicting a group of individuals sitting in a hotel lobby as her heroine, a journalist, arrives in Prague just as Hitler is about to occupy Czechoslovakia. She describes how they are sat around a table strewn with glasses; all looked as though they drank heavily, even if they did not, and were instantly recognisable as a group of foreign correspondents. Gellhorn writes:

> They had met for years now, in various capitals, in trains and boats and on odd roads. They were warmly intimate and affectionate with each other, though sometimes pompous too ... sometimes flirtatious in order to rest the mind and change the conversation, sometimes honest because after all they were people working on the same job, needing help or advice.

Gellhorn's novel captures camaraderie among foreign correspondents in the field, dependent on one another for the company but equally each seeking the chance to sneak off on their own to secure an exclusive story that will not be shared. *Washington Post* reporters Bob Woodward and Carl Bernstein certainly did not share the identity of their Watergate source "Deep Throat" with rival newsrooms and in the early days of social media, it was standard practice that newspapers, as they moved online, would routinely hold back scoops until late in the evening so as not to tip off rivals. History and novels aside, today's agency journalism displays some intense rivalries, not least between Reuters and Bloomberg where competition in recent years has been little short of bitter. And as the social media guidelines issued to agency journalists show, breaking news belongs on the normal news wire for paying clients first, not on a platform for everyone to share.

But times are changing. Large-scale data leaks in today's digital world have seen a new form of collaborative journalism emerge, partly reflecting the shift towards a networked news environment, but partly out of pure necessity. These leaks, often of sensitive political or financial information, contain overwhelming amounts of data and require intense follow-up investigation. Borges-Rey argues that a new approach is needed (2016: 833):

> An emergent breed of data journalists, empowered by the methods and tools of data science, begins to display a remarkable understanding of the computing language and logics behind this datafication of the world, making apparent a growing need to revise many of the traditional practices and philosophies of the news media establishment.

In 2015, the Munich-based German daily *Süddeutsche Zeitung* received a leak of 11.5 million documents relating to offshore investments which became known as the "Panama Papers"; a second leak to two reporters on the same newspaper about a year later included 13.4 million documents on a similar subject and became known as the "Paradise Papers." The *Süddeutsche Zeitung* shared the material in both instances with the International Consortium of Investigative Journalists (ICIJ) in Washington DC, a global network of 280 investigative reporters from more than 100 countries and territories.[6] The Panama Papers files were described by Edward Snowden as "the biggest leak in the history of data journalism."[7] The files came from Mossack Fonseca, a law firm based in Panama with branches in Hong Kong, Zurich and dozens of other places. As ICIJ's Will Fitzgibbon and Michael Hudson wrote in a review of the operation, the firm's leaked internal files contained information on 214,488 offshore entities connected to people in more than 200 countries and territories (2021). This included e-mails, financial spreadsheets, passports and corporate records revealing the secret owners of bank accounts and companies in 21 outposts in the offshore system, from Nevada to the British Virgin Islands. The Panama Papers would, they wrote, "become a byword for exposing financial chicanery and political corruption." More than 370 journalists from 76 news organisations across six continents worked on the project in secret for more than a year before the first stories were published in April 2016. The revelations of widespread tax fraud, political and financial corruption won a Pulitzer Prize in 2017 and have proved to be a model for international collaboration to tackle such data leaks. As Lewis observes (2018: 11):

> Some of the most outstanding public service journalism certainly has benefited enormously from technologically enabled, multimedia collaborations *between* various news organisation bureaus, as well as editorial coordination and communication on a heretofore

unimaginably large scale on important, exceedingly difficult, timely news-making projects.

Far from being the first such investigation, the Panama Papers was the 26th coordinated by the ICIJ. It had emerged from one of the pioneers of collaborative work as a project of the Centre for Public Integrity and became a separate non-profit organisation in 2017. In Britain, the non-profit Bureau of Investigative Journalism, established in 2010, works on a similar collaborative model. Recent investigations have focused on threats to the Amazon rainforest from the global beef industry (with Repórter Brasil), US covert warfare operations (with the *New York Times*) and the COVID-19 pandemic. Such collaborations enable a sophisticated technological analysis of data with specialist software applications and specialisation in data analysis, spread the burden of reporting across news organisations and allow in-depth investigation into specific strands of data that may apply to just one country or its institutions. In addition, the actual act of collaboration and publishing simultaneously across the globe can in itself be news, increasing the impact of the journalism (Sambrook, 2018: 1).

Even here, however, the news organisations collaborating on such projects do not entirely set aside their competitive instincts. Sambrook's analysis of collaborative journalism shows that such instincts need to be carefully managed. In the case of the Panama and Paradise Papers, the ICIJ played the role of a trusted and neutral intermediary, nurturing partnerships in a non-competitive way (2018: 28). There are clearly tensions, not least because partners – broadcasters, newspapers, online only and other media outlets – have very different schedules ranging from weekly to daily and minute by minute. He added:

> A neutral partner – such as a non-profit news organisation or jointly owned joint venture – can play a valuable role in managing tensions and potential conflicts of interest between partners. In the end, one trusted party has to make decisions and hold other partners to account.

News agencies have, of course, carried out their own investigations from the very beginning of their history and have always pulled together networks of journalists to work with them as stringers, freelancers or fixers. But generally, the agencies have not joined forces with those leading the collaborative approach practised by the likes of the ICIJ. To date, Reuters has preferred to conduct its own investigations but has signalled it is open to the right collaborations. As the controversy at Reuters over the quest for Pulitzer prizes shows, the model of time-consuming international investigations is for some at odds with the culture of breaking news. A commentary in The Baron discussion forum reflected concerns that the agency was being distracted from its core business of producing fast-breaking news and jeopardising its subscriber base (2021a):

> There is concern that the Reuters brand has lost prestige because of a retreat from its traditional supremacy in this area. Long-form special reports may win prizes and enhance Reuters reputation with other media, especially in the United States, but they do not pay any bills.

The concerns at Reuters stem directly from the perceived danger to breaking news and competitive timings in the financial markets against arch rival Bloomberg. One senior journalist at Reuters said there were clearly times when it was appropriate for the agency to engage in investigative journalism but there was no reason to "throw the baby out with the bathwater" and undermine the core discipline of breaking news. As such, what do about investigative journalism is one of the challenges facing Reuters new Editor-in-Chief Alessandra Galloni. In her first months in charge, she signalled that speed cannot be sacrificed. In a message to staff, she spoke about how the Reuters newsroom would be (cited in The Baron, 2021b):

> Speedy and smart, leveraging a global footprint with local expertise to drive coverage of the most important stories in the world, for the world, without bias, both in real time and in depth, and with sophistication and insight. How do we do this? With a rigorous focus on breaking news and beat reporting.

The issue has been less problematic for AP, which focuses much more on "general news" and its investigations team has a track record of carrying out Pulitzer Prize-winning long-term research into complex stories. Equally, AFP has at times engaged in longer-form journalism, recently producing a series of multi-media reports on the West African nomadic Fulani people. But AFP's Chetwynd is clear that there is a strategic danger in trying to do too much in a media landscape that is continually evolving and long-form stories have to be chosen carefully. It was simply not realistic, he said, to assign reporters to a project for six months or more at a time when clients are more concerned with day-to-day news coverage.

A community-based approach

A number of organisations have also built up global networks of reporters that take on the characteristics of an international news agency but with a slightly different agenda that tends to privilege a form of activism and empathic reporting. Two examples explored in this section of the chapter are *Global Voices*, a non-profit news organisation that draws on a community approach and grassroots citizens media, and the *Institute for War & Peace Reporting* (IWPR) that is engaged in capacity building for local journalism, supporting independent media specifically in nations in conflict, crisis or transition.[8]

Global Voices was established in 2005 by former CNN Beijing and Tokyo Bureau Chief Rebecca MacKinnon and technologist and Africa expert Ethan Zuckerman while they were both fellows at the Berkman Center for Internet and Society at Harvard University. It is founded on the principle of the right to free speech and is a large volunteer community that operates worldwide without the traditional infrastructure of offices. It defines free speech as "protecting the right to speak – and the right to listen"[9] and emphasises how, using digital tools, it can break the stranglehold of established media and governments on the flow of information:

> Thanks to new tools, speech need no longer be controlled by those who own the means of publishing and distribution, or by governments that would restrict thought and communication. Now, anyone can wield the power of the press. Everyone can tell their stories to the world.

Global Voices aims to meet this objective by verifying and translating trending news and stories that might not be seen on mainstream platforms using blogs, independent press and social media around the world. Its goal is therefore to discover, contextualise and translate international stories (Villa & Fowler-Watt, 2018), including in its community not only local journalists but also academics and human rights activists. This situates *Global Voices* somewhere between the work a news agency might perform (in gathering and verifying third-party material) and alternative media (in that it embraces activists). It is keen to emphasise the differences, trying to re-balance the media landscape and correct shortcomings in the professional media's coverage of the developing world, namely, an overreliance on uninformed "parachute journalists."[10] As part of this, it seeks to avoid crisis reporting with its emphasis on natural disasters and conflict, instead prioritising more complex and long-term stories that allow the voices of those directly affected to be heard (Zuckerman, 2013: 217). As such, *Global Voices* comes closer to Berglez's definition of a global journalism and, as its Executive Director Ivan Sigal says, it does not seek to impose editorial values (Sigal, 2019):

> We've long espoused the ideal that online spaces are spaces for conversation and spaces for people to learn from each other across cultures and across languages and we've always tried to live that ideal as well.

A case in point is *Global Voices's* handling of the Syrian conflict which tends to have been viewed elsewhere in polarised terms, pitting pro-Assad voices such as the Russian 24-hour news channel RT against Western news outlets which have sometimes relied on parachute journalism and reports from those in rebel-held areas. Sigal explains how multiple sources can be accessed to build up a detailed and differentiated understanding, drawing on the millions of images, videos, blogs, tweets and audio files that have been created about the war. But he adds a cautionary note that manipulation and disinformation have become weaponised as part of the conflict. For *Global Voices*, that places an emphasis on verification that is no different from that practised by mainstream news outlets and the agencies. He states (2016):

> Against the forces of misinformation, finding and building coherent narratives about the war is an immense challenge. We now know the principles and techniques for organizing, prioritizing and verifying information coming out of Syria. We can identify facts and establish evidence through careful analysis, and with media forensics techniques such as reverse image search, geolocation and metadata analysis. We can build and maintain trusted relationships with friends, colleagues and sources who are proximate to the conflict.

IWPR also has a tradition of working in conflict zones, building capacity in a democratic media and drawing on project funding from major Western development agencies. It has an activist goal of driving change but also adheres to fundamental values of journalism, emphasising verification, transparency and freedom from bias. Its international network of local journalists is supported through specific project funding and cannot emulate the minute-by-minute global coverage of news agencies. But the focus on local voices and their local perspective provides a valuable picture of life in conflict zones that is complementary to mainstream Western media. IWPR's projects range from Africa and Asia to Latin America and the Middle East and include training to detect and combat disinformation, strengthen independent reporting networks and support women's organisations. In the years following the Taliban's initial defeat at the hands of US-led forces in 2001, IWPR trained and supported thousands of journalists in Afghanistan but also, following its remit of capacity building, worked with civil society leaders and young people to promote transitional justice, good governance and human rights. Today, its ability to report out of Afghanistan is threatened and IWPR's former country Director Noorrahman Rahmani was forced to flee with his family in 2021, taking with him just a bag of clothes. "Afghanistan's flourishing media scene," he wrote from exile, "one of our greatest achievements, is in particular danger."

The London-based Bureau of Investigative Journalism actively seeks to drive change and treads a narrow line between that and advocacy as it engages with communities. One of its former journalists Ben Du Preez explained that for the Bureau's journalism to do its job effectively it needs to go beyond a "publish-and-hope-for-the-best" approach (i.e. beyond the plain vanilla journalism of the news agencies). This, he said, means embracing impact as a goal without campaigning for a particular outcome. Instead, the aim is to equip campaigners with the information *they* can use (2020). The collaborative journalism networks have also focused on community reporting and, in emphasising local reporting, distanced themselves from parachute journalism, privileging instead listening to those being interviewed. Du Preez outlined the Bureau's concerns about what he called "extractive journalism" techniques used by mainstream Western news outlets where success is measured by a story's reach:

> Time and again, they (journalists) would parachute in, extract what they or their editors deemed "valuable," relay it to an audience elsewhere, only to be next seen again picking up shiny individual gongs for their work highlighting these systemic abuses.
>
> Time and again, they would unwittingly perpetuate the very power imbalances they sought to expose, reducing people to "case studies," stripping them of agency and giving them no control over how they were represented.

The community approach to international journalism thus places a high value on empathy and concern for the mental wellbeing of those caught up in disaster or conflict and begs the question whether mainstream Western news organisations are guilty of such extraction journalism. A case in point has been mounting criticism of the way British broadcast media outlets have covered the wave of migrants crossing the English Channel from France. In August 2020, the BBC and Sky filmed flimsy boats packed with migrants as they navigated the perilous crossing, prompting the Labour Party member of parliament Zarah Sultana to say (cited in Waterson, 2020):

> We should ensure people don't drown crossing the Channel, not film them as if it were some grotesque reality TV show.

It can be argued that the international news agencies have been in a good position to avoid the worst excesses of parachute journalism by having foreign correspondents stationed for long-term postings (often three to five years) in overseas bureaux where they develop local knowledge, local sources and work together with locally recruited journalists (sometimes disparagingly called "local staff"[11]). But given recent budget cuts and the slimming down of some foreign bureaux, they too often need to fly in additional journalists from head office to cover major breaking news stories. Difficult scenes of human suffering raised deep concerns at AFP in 2015 as its reporters and photographers covered the wave of migrants fleeing the Syrian conflict and trying to enter Europe through the Greek islands. The harrowing pictures that captured the lifeless body of a Syrian toddler, Alan Kurdi, who drowned trying to reach the Greek island of Kos, caused shock waves worldwide. The suffering of the migrants also had a profound impact on the journalists covering the refugee story, some of whom were hardened war correspondents. This time, however, they were not in a war zone, mentally prepared for what they were to witness, but on Greek islands which would otherwise be a holiday destination. This incongruity was highlighted by AFP's global Editor-in-Chief Phil Chetwynd who was quoted as saying in a study on journalism and moral injury[12] (cited in Feinstein & Storm, 2017: 8):

> The thing people have found very hard is that there is no danger to you at all, yet you're watching boats being overturned and people drowning.

Sometimes photographers dropped their cameras and waded into the water to help the migrants ashore. What did that mean for the role of the journalist as a dispassionate, neutral observer? Chetwynd was clear where AFP stood (ibid: 17):

> We came to the conclusion that we did formally have to say to our journalists in our charter that you are a human being, you are more than a journalist and therefore the instinct to put your camera down and help a child out the water or to buy a pizza or whatever may be completely natural ... it's not realistic or feasible to try to stick to some very rigid idea of trying to be some sort of neutral observer under these circumstances, and yet the question can be where do you put the cursor because once you creep over that, you can get extremely involved ... ultimately, you are talking about human beings on the ground managing their own situations.

Agencies, such as Reuters and AFP, have been keen to support the mental wellbeing of their own reporting staff, acutely aware that they can often be exposed to distressing scenes. Reuters introduced its first support for its journalists shortly before the 2003 war against Iraq, supported by the Dart Centre for Journalism & Trauma,[13] and provided external counselling and peer support. AP, CNN and the BBC did the same. But the subject has also proved to be controversial and there have been signs that job cuts have increased stress over and beyond that associated with covering distressing news stories. One of Reuters journalists Dean Yates, a former Baghdad Bureau Chief who himself had been diagnosed with PTSD,[14] became an advocate within the agency for mental health care in 2017[15] but resigned three years later, asserting that the agency had not done enough to address gaps in its provision and care for journalists.

Do the soft power players change anything?

While the collaborative networks and community-based outlets such as *Global Voices* are harnessing digital technologies and social media in an attempt to go beyond the dominant Western view of the world, a new generation of state-owned broadcast outlets is using tried and tested 24-hour news formats to shine a different perspective on the news. Some of these channels, particularly those based in Western Europe, adhere to traditional views of objectivity and impartiality. Others can at best be viewed as an attempt to wield soft power and at worst an exercise in crude propaganda and malicious disinformation.

The state-owned broadcaster France-24 was born out of the frustration at the dominant Western view of the world purveyed by the news agencies, CNN and the BBC. It was founded in 2006 on exactly the same values of objectivity and impartiality but seeks to redress their agenda setting and framing of the news, stating it offers a French perspective and "comprehensive coverage of world events, with a focus on cultural diversity and contrasting viewpoints via news bulletins, reports, magazines and debates." The project was the brainchild of President Jacques Chirac who vented his anger and a feeling in France that the nation needed greater international presence in the media to put its views across in the build-up to the 2003 Gulf War. In 2002, he re-launched a project that had been first mooted in 1987, saying:

> The recent crises have shown the handicap that a country suffers, a cultural area, which doesn't possess a sufficient weight in the battle of the images and the airwaves. Let us question, in the time of terrestrial television networks, of satellite, of the internet, on our organisation in this domain, and notably in the dissipation of public funds which are reserved to them.

France-24 broadcast first in French and English, later adding Arabic and Spanish. However, tight budgets have limited its ability to report globally and any alternative French perspective and values have been most evident in cultural and lifestyle programming (Painter, 2008: 14). Far older channels, such as Deutsche Welle (state-owned with roots dating back to 1953) and Euronews (a pan-European network dating back to 1993 which is owned by European state broadcasters and Media Globe Networks), are similar attempts to provide a different perspective while retaining the dominant Western objectivity paradigm.

By contrast, CGTN, RT and Iran's Press TV are clear voices of their respective governments (although they sometimes argue that this is not the case) and have had several confrontations with European broadcasting regulators. All three aim to counter the dominant Western media narrative and see the concept of impartiality as a cover for Western hegemonic power (Painter, 2008: 9). CGTN's coverage of China's tightening of control over Hong Kong reflects the Beijing view while Western media have tended to focus on the rolling back of Hong's traditional freedoms. RT has consistently covered the Syrian conflict from a perspective of the Russian-backed Assad government in contrast to the mainstream Western media narrative that has sometimes reported more from the rebel perspective.

Collaboration, community and state actors 99

RT, launched in 2005 as Russia Today, broadcasts in Russian, English, Spanish and Arabic and, sparking controversy, launched RT America in 2010 to target a US audience. A year later, the then U.S. Secretary of State Hillary Clinton warned the Senate Foreign Relations Committee that the United States was losing an information war at the hands of Arabic news channels and English-language programming from China and Russia. She said:

> During the Cold War, we did a great job in getting America's message out. After the Berlin Wall fell we said, 'okay, fine, enough of that. We've done it. We're done.' And unfortunately, we are paying a big price for it. And our private media cannot fill that gap ...
>
> So, we are in an information war. And we are losing that war. I'll be very blunt in my assessment. Al-Jazeera is winning. The Chinese have opened up a global English-language and multi-language television network. The Russians have opened up an English-language network. I've seen it in a few countries, and it's quite instructive. We are cutting back. The BBC is cutting back.

In 2014 in the United States, one of RT's Washington-based anchors, Liz Wahl, resigned on air, accusing the network of whitewashing Russia's military intervention in Ukraine. Setting aside her script, she said:

> I cannot be part of a network funded by the Russian government that whitewashes the actions of Putin. I'm proud to be an American and believe in disseminating the truth, and that is why, after this newscast, I'm resigning.

In 2019 in the United Kingdom, RT was fined £200,000 by the British regulator Ofcom having been found to have breached its broadcast code seven times in six weeks following the poisoning of the former Russian military officer Sergei Skripal and his daughter Yulia in the cathedral city of Salisbury.[16] Ofcom concluded that RT programmes breached rules on impartiality, including the Salisbury poisonings and coverage of Syria that presented only a pro-Russian viewpoint. RT subsequently challenged the Ofcom ruling in the English High Court, arguing that the dominant media view at the time was that Russia was to blame – it was therefore legitimate for RT to limit its Salisbury coverage to the Russian view (that the Kremlin was not behind the poisonings) and leave out other views. The High Court upheld Ofcom's ruling, however, with Lord Justice Dingemans saying it was of paramount importance for media to be balanced in an era of fake news.

Iran's state-controlled Press TV started broadcasting in 2007 but lost its UK licence in 2012 after Ofcom established that editorial operations were directed from Tehran, a clear breach of its rules. Critics have called it pro-Palestinian, anti-Semitic, anti-American and a propaganda platform for the Iranian government. CGTN had until recently steered relatively clear of regulatory problems but also lost its UK broadcasting licence in 2021 after Ofcom decided that the channel was ultimately controlled by the Chinese Communist Party in Beijing. CGTN's coverage of Hong Kong and the broadcasting of false confessions from detainees had also come under increased scrutiny. The state broadcaster has, however, established major editorial hubs in London, Nairobi and Washington DC, part of a multi-billion-dollar investment in China's state-run media to expand its presence abroad, including the official news agency Xinhua, China Radio International and state newspapers *China Daily* and *People's Daily*. They all have three things in common: they are well-known media in their native China, they are government owned, and they represent the official voice (Si, 2014: 3). Commenting on China's goals of soft power shortly after the launch of CCTV America in 2012 from the new Washington studios, *Columbia Journalism Review* wrote (2012):

> The Communist Party hopes to remake the negative image of China that it perceives in coverage by Western broadcasters. It hopes to replace the images of urban pollution, self-immolating Tibetan monks, and sweatshop workers with those of its rapidly growing cities and a prosperous new consumer class.

Of all the soft-power broadcasters, CGTN has expanded its network of foreign bureaux the most, emulating the structure of Western news organisations and hiring Western correspondents and anchors to try to deflect criticism that it is just a propaganda machine.

Conclusion

The alternative approaches to international journalism explored in this chapter represent a realisation that in today's networked environment the news agenda can be pushed beyond the limits of what is routinely provided by the daily feeds from mainstream Western news agencies and broadcasters. But to what extent have these approaches succeeded in rebalancing the hegemonic news agenda of the West and in reducing the news agencies' iron grip on gatekeeping?

The collaborative approach typified by the work of the International Consortium of Investigative Journalists is driven in part by technical necessity. Large-scale data leaks[17] require collaborative investigative teams that can use sophisticated technological tools and drill down into stories in individual countries. While this is undoubtedly within the capability of the news agencies – and indeed resembles their structure – it runs counter to the agencies' instinct to cover breaking news, it drains resources and risks jeopardising the core business. The community-based approach espoused by *Global Voices* is symptomatic of a deep frustration with the dominant Western framing of the news agenda and an attempt to harness the power of social media to tap into other voices. Many of these approaches are not-for-profit and operate within the Western value system of impartiality and holding power to account. But crucially they sometimes go beyond the plain vanilla journalism of the news agencies to pursue direct impact and can embrace activists, NGOs and advocacy organisations. The state-controlled actors seeking to rebalance the news agenda are clearly divided into two camps, those which also adhere to core Western journalistic values, such as France-24 and Euronews, and those which aim to promote their government's view of the world, such as RT, Press TV and CGTN.

When it comes to the collaborative and community networks which have emerged, the reporting can best be described as complementary to the mainstream Western news agenda. The in-depth investigations of the Panama, Paradise and Pandora Papers perform the classic function of holding power to account, exposing corruption and financial chicanery. Such organisations as the ICIJ enlist the support of journalists often seconded from mainstream news organisations and employ journalistic norms that are typical of the major news agencies, BBC or CNN. The community approach taken by the likes of *Global Voices* and IWPR does succeed in giving a platform to voices that might otherwise remain unheard and avoids the excesses of a crude extractive journalism that generates a quick news "hit." This shift away from legacy news organisations goes some way to generating a greater diversity of views and countering the inherent Western bias in mainstream outlets. But their relatively limited distribution and low profile means that they remain a complementary source of news in the margins.

State-controlled broadcasters such as France-24 which adhere to Western journalism principles have been hamstrung by lack of finance and their influence has often been limited to diaspora audiences seeking a perspective from their own home country. As for broadcasters such as RT and CGTN, their ability to deliver a different perspective on the news and break the Western hegemony has been seriously undermined by their political agendas. Analysis of RT together with the Russian news agency and radio station Sputnik by King's College London concluded that they perform a "damage control" function for the Russian state during incidents such as the poisoning of Sergei and Yulia Skripal and deploy a range of tactics to project Russian strength and construct news agendas (Ramsay & Robertshaw, 2019: 6). While this is hardly surprising, more worrying is the analysis that UK tabloid newspapers have been lifting small numbers of RT and Sputnik stories and incorporating them into their online reporting. Though a content analysis of 12,000 articles showed that this practice was not widespread, the authors characterised it as "needless and indefensible, particularly in the cases identified where information regarding Russian military policy or about the Skripal poisoning was replicated without attribution and presented to audiences" (ibid: 101). The analysis shows that a news operation such as RT plays fast and loose with journalistic standards and has little in common with attempts to harness citizens' voices or bring about a greater understanding of issues through community journalism. Rather, they are part of the current landscape of disinformation and propaganda. Unfortunately, sanctions against broadcasters, such as RT and CGTN, have led to tit-for-tat retaliation against Western journalists in Moscow and Beijing.

Viewed as a whole, these approaches to journalism provide at best a complementary perspective to the powerful agenda setting of the news agencies and key global news organisations. While they may have made some inroads into the traditional flow of information from the North to the South, they have by no means reversed it and remain in the margins of today's digital news environment. The traditional gatekeepers are still the dominant force.

Notes

1. The international operations of the Chinese state broadcaster CCTV were rebranded in 2016 as China Global Television Network or CGTN.
2. The station was launched as Russia Today in 2005 and rebranded as RT in 2009.
3. See: https://cnnpressroom.blogs.cnn.com/cnn-fact-sheet/
4. See Chapter 1, p. 26, for a discussion of the UNESCO report in relation to major news agencies.

5. See Chapter 1, p. 20, for a discussion of the agencies news alliance.
6. See: https://www.icij.org/
7. See: https://twitter.com/Snowden/status/716683740903247873
8. The author is a long-standing trustee of IWPR.
9. See Global Voices manifesto: https://globalvoices.org/about/gv-manifesto/
10. A parachute journalist is a reporter who flies into a country to cover a story at short-notice. The implication in what is a derogatory term is that he or she will have little prior knowledge of the country or story. This means the story is likely to be framed from their Western perspective. By contrast, a local journalist or foreign correspondent who has been posted to a country for a number of years can be expected to be better informed.
11. See discussion in Chapter 2, p. 52 on AP's phasing out of expatriate packages for foreign correspondents.
12. The concept of moral injury denotes the harm that may arise when people witness things that transgress their expectations of a just and morally ordered society. It takes on particular significance because of the nature of journalism (Browne, Evangeli, & Greenberg, 2012: 207): "Journalists ... are a unique cohort, distinct from other high-risk groups in that they often experience or witness traumatic events, but are not expected to intervene. Not having a direct, helping role when attending to traumatic incidents may present journalists with complex ethical dilemmas. For example, morally believing the right thing to do is to provide aid, versus the knowledge that one should remain objective."
13. The author is a trustee and former chair of the Dart Centre for Journalism & Trauma in Europe. The charity provides support for journalists suffering from stress incurred through coverage of traumatic news stories; it also provides best practice guidelines and resources for what I call trauma-literate reporting by promoting better understanding of issues around trauma.
14. Post-traumatic stress disorder (PTSD) was formally diagnosed as a condition in 1980. It is mainly used in connection with situations which actual death, injury and sexual assault, or the threat of these. When it comes to journalists, indirect exposure, for example repeated exposure to witnessing and reporting on traumatic events, is recognised in the medical literature as a potential vector for harm.
15. Dean Yates talks about his experiences, his diagnosis of PTSD and issues of moral injury in a 2017 interview with the *Columbia Journalism Review*. See: https://www.cjr.org/the_profile/dean-yates-reuters-ptsd.php
16. Sergei Skripal was a double agent working for British intelligence agencies. He and his daughter were poisoned with the nerve agent Novichok in March 2018. The British government, backed by an alliance of 28 other countries, accused Russia of attempted murder and expelled a number of Russian diplomats.
17. The latest, called the "Pandora Papers," contained almost 12 million documents.

References

Allan, S., 2013. *Citizen witnessing: Revisioning journalism in times of crisis*. Cambridge: Polity Press.

Berglez, P., 2008. What is global journalism? Theoretical and empirical conceptualisations. *Journalism Studies*, 9(6), pp. 845–858.

Borges-Rey, E., 2016. Unravelling data journalism: A study of data journalism practice in British newsrooms. *Journalism Practice*, 10(7), pp. 833–843.

Browne, T., Evangeli, M., and Greenberg, N., 2012. Trauma-related guilt and posttraumatic stress among journalists. *Journal of Traumatic Stress*, 25(2), pp. 207–210.

Bruns, A., 2003. Gatewatching not gatekeeping: Collaborative online news. *Media International Australia Incorporating Culture and Policy: Quarterly Journal of Media Research and Resources*, 107, pp. 31–44.

Bruns, A., 2011. News produsage in a pro-am mediassphere: Why citizen journalism matters. In Meikle, G. & Redden, G. (Eds.), *News online: Transformations and continuities*. Basingstoke: Palgrave MacMillan.

Columbia Journalism Review. 2012. Sino the times—Can China's billions buy media credibility? https://archives.cjr.org/feature/sino_the_times.php

Cottle, S., 2009. Preface. In Allan, S. and Thorsen, E. (Eds.), *Citizen journalism: Global perspectives* (Vol. 1). New York: Peter Lang.

Du Preez, B. 2020. The problem with extractive journalism. *Bureau of Investigative Journalism*, 12 August 2020. https://www.thebureauinvestigates.com/blog/2020-08-12/the-problem-with-extractive-journalism

Feinstein, A. and Storm, H. 2017. The emotional toll on journalists covering the refugee crisis. https://reutersinstitute.politics.ox.ac.uk/sites/default/files/2017-07/Storm%20and%20Feinstein%20-%20Emotional%20Toll.pdf

Fitzgibbon, W. and Hudson, M. 2021. Five years later, Panama Papers still having a big impact. International Consortium of Investigative Journalists. https://www.icij.org/investigations/panama-papers/five-years-later-panama-papers-still-having-a-big-impact/

Gellhorn, M., 1940. *A stricken field: A novel*. Chicago: University of Chicago Press.

Lewis, C., 2018. Tear down these walls: Innovations in collaborative accountability research and reporting. In Sambrook, R. (Ed.), *Global teamwork: the rise of collaboration in investigative journalism*. Oxford: Reuters Institute for the Study of Journalism.

Painter, J., 2008. *Counter-hegemonic news: A case study of Al-Jazeera English and Telesûr*. Reuters Institute for the Study of Journalism. Oxford: University of Oxford.

Porwancher, A., 2011. Objectivity's prophet: Adolph S Ochs and the New York times 1896–1935. *Journalism History*, 36(4), pp. 186–195.

Rai, M. and Cottle, S., 2007. Global mediations: On the changing ecology of satellite television news. *Global Media and Communication*, 3(1), pp. 51–78.

Ramsay, G. and Robertshaw, S., 2019. *Weaponising news: RT, sputnik and targeted disinformation*. London: Kings College London.

Sambrook, R. (Ed). 2018. *Global teamwork: The rise of collaboration in investigative journalism.* Oxford: Reuters Institute for the Study of Journalism.

Si, S., 2014. *Expansion of international broadcasting.* Working paper, Reuters Institute for the Study of Journalism.

Sigal, I. 2016. Syria's war may be the most documented ever. And yet, we know so little. https://www.pri.org/stories/2016-12-19/syrias-war-may-be-most-documented-ever-and-yet-we-know-so-little

Sigal, I. 2019. Global voices asks its contributors to make its strategic decisions instead of a boardroom. *Journalism.com*, 1 February 2019. https://www.journalism.co.uk/podcast/how-global-voices-is-asking-their-contributors-to-inform-some-of-their-biggest-decisions/s399/a734071/

The Baron, 2021a. Will Reuters new editor bring change or more of the same? *The Baron*, 19 April 2021. https://www.thebaron.info/editorial/will-reuters-new-editor-bring-change-or-more-of-the-same

The Baron, 2021b. Reuters chief changes top team in drive for "speedy and smart" newsroom. *The Baron*, 30 August 2021. https://thebaron.info/news/article/2021/08/30/reuters-chief-changes-top-team-in-drive-for-speedy-and-smart-newsroom

Thussu, D.K., 2003. Live TV and bloodless deaths: War, infotainment and 24/7 news. In Thussu, D.K. & Freedman, D. (Eds.), *War and the media, reporting conflict 24/7*. London: Sage.

Villa, M.K. and Fowler-Watt, K. 2018. Reporting refugees: An analysis of global voices. Unpublished paper.

Volkmer, I., 1999. *News in the global sphere: A study of CNN and its impact on global communication.* Luton: University of Luton Press.

Volkmer, I., 2003. The global network society and the global public sphere. *Development*, 46(1), pp. 9–16.

Waterson, J. 2020. BBC and Sky accused of "voyeurism" in coverage of migrant boats. *The Guardian*, 11 August, 2020. https://www.theguardian.com/uk-news/2020/aug/11/bbc-and-sky-accused-of-dehumanising-people-trying-to-cross-channel

Williams, K., 2011. *International journalism*. London: Sage.

Zuckerman, E., 2013. *Digital cosmopolitans: why we think the Internet connects us, why it doesn't and how to rewire it.* New York: W.W. Norton & Company.

Conclusion
News agencies – rooted in the past and looking to the future

> The flow of information from fax machines to the Internet and through other technologies already developed or still undreamed of will overwhelm efforts to control it. Today and in the future, anyone sending information from one country to another is a *de facto* foreign correspondent.
>
> Garrick Utley, Foreign Affairs, 1997

Introduction

The veteran US foreign correspondent Garrick Utley could hardly have known how prophetic his words would be when he wrote an article in 1997 for *Foreign Affairs* about the state of international news gathering. In an era before social media, Facebook, Twitter and Instagram, Utley, whose 40-year career spanned the mighty American networks NBC, ABC and CNN, foresaw the seismic changes sending tremors through the news industry. Utley was documenting the technological and financial pressures emerging at the end of the 20th century which would lead to the inexorable decline of the US television networks' overseas presence. But he could just as well have been outlining the challenges to the international news agencies, which had been synonymous with foreign news gathering for the previous 150 years. What would later become commonly known as social media, citizen journalism and user-generated content was to weaken established media's grip on the news agenda, calling into question the very role of the foreign correspondent and prompting the news agencies and other global news outlets to re-valuate both their editorial and business strategies.

This book has explored in the past chapters how the news agencies have attempted to retain their relevance in the global news industry, drawing both on their long heritage of fact-based news values while at

DOI: 10.4324/9781003029656-6

the same time trying to adapt to the ever-shifting news landscape and the unprecedented scale of disruption. Their retrenchment overseas has been far less dramatic than that of the American television networks or major newspapers and they, like other news organisations, have been able to draw on social media content for their reporting. But the first two decades of the 21st century have also been marked by stringent cost cutting at the agencies and a reduction in some of their overseas news gathering operations, particularly at AP and Reuters. Questions are being asked whether this has gone too far and might have jeopardised their core strength. Around the world, the news agencies have seen their traditional customer base eroded as mainstream media outlets come under sustained financial pressure and so have been unable to avoid an inevitable squeeze on editorial budgets. The attempts to capture new markets and add retail customers to the traditional wholesale client base have encountered mixed success but an instinctive focus on fact-based journalism and verification services has underscored their credentials and begun to pay dividends. In the face of social media, the agencies have shown no sign of compromising on their long-held news values and have demonstrated a dogged determination not to give up their status as gatekeepers. On the contrary, their expansion of verification operations illustrates their resolve to be arbiters of what is "proper" news and what is not.

Are there winners and losers in this period of disruption? Clearly, the upstart new(ish) player Bloomberg has continued to make inroads into the once powerful dominance of Reuters in providing financial news to the markets, at times clearly to its staff's frustration and embarrassment. Bloomberg's £1 billion showpiece London headquarters is typical of its brash attitude and testimony to its business confidence. AFP has also emerged as a winner as it challenges and makes inroads into what was once a duopoly of Reuters and AP as providers of television footage to wholesale broadcast clients. All the agencies have ploughed additional resources into verification. Partly, this reflects the deep-seated culture of the agencies and the fact that, classically defined, journalism is a practice of verification (Broersma & Graham, 2013: 461; Kovach, 2010). Partly, it represents the desire to capture new business opportunities as partnerships are forged with some of the social media platforms such as Facebook. AP and Reuters have registered public success with a series of Pulitzer prizes both for textual reporting and their news photography. But what is second nature to AP has raised concerns within Reuters that the discipline of fast breaking news has taken second place to longer-form investigative journalism.

This chapter attempts to determine what has changed in the past two decades, what has remained constant and where the greatest threats and opportunities lie.

The last outpost

Utley's fateful prediction about the decline of foreign news gathering has more or less become fact. As the award-winning conflict journalist Janine di Giovanni has written, the type of reporting and photojournalism that typified coverage of the Vietnam War, with the likes of Peter Arnett and Don McCullin of the *Sunday Times*, has almost disappeared (2021). The decline of foreign news gathering came in stages, she has argued, partly with the control over stories exercised through the system of embedding during the 2003 Iraq war and partly with the dominance of 24/7 television news channels which resulted in correspondents being "chained to the satellite dish" and unable to report original material from the field. The decisive blow came with the 2008 global financial crisis that led to remaining budgets for foreign news coverage being cut still further. This is not just a matter of nostalgia for a bygone age. As Giovanni notes, there are serious societal consequences (2021):

> Without a solid basis in deeply reported, well-sourced facts from around the globe as a counterweight to the social media-driven flood of narratives, opinion, and disinformation, it becomes ever more difficult to have an informed public debate about foreign-policy choices.

The Syrian conflict, she concludes, is a case in point, where public debate has been shaped almost entirely by second- and third-hand information, opinionating pundits, and social media. Why should anyone bother going to dangerous, expensive Aleppo when you can tweet your take from your desk in your bathrobe, she asks.

Today, the international news agencies are to all intents and purposes the last outpost of foreign news reporting. The generous remuneration packages of the past for the privileged class of expatriate foreign correspondents (school fees, private health insurance, return flights home each year and company housing) have generally been phased out but news organisations around the world still rely on the news agencies for breaking news stories from overseas. The agencies are all too aware that this is one of their major selling points. Despite cut-backs, AP states that it has a reporting presence in 250 locations worldwide, Reuters speaks of more than 200 locations, AFP has staff in 151 countries and

Bloomberg counts more than 150 bureaux. Only global giants such as the *New York Times* can come anywhere close to matching that type of network. Today, each of the agencies promotes its foreign news gathering network with slick marketing slogans: AP speaks of "news and services that expand the reach of factual reporting," Bloomberg prides itself in "trusted and extensive coverage of global markets." In AFP's annual report, global news director Chetwynd makes a point of emphasising how the French agency has maintained a comprehensive network of correspondents across the world (2021):

> At AFP, we believe we have access to one of the biggest and most complete networks of journalists in the world. Our feeling is that our competitors pulled back some journalists from places that maybe they don't think are important. On the contrary, we've always subscribed to the idea that stories can happen anywhere and that, as such, it is impossible to know where the most important places are in terms of positioning your network.

That pointed comment is primarily a diplomatic allusion to the slimming down of AP's network and, in turn, highlights AFP's policy not to reduce its overseas presence. But it could equally apply to Reuters where there has been public discontent among its journalists in the face of cuts that have seen a particular erosion of staff on foreign language services, once a strength in local reporting that fed the international news wire. That discontent was captured in *Le Monde*'s discussion of the effective halving of staff on the Reuters French desk in Paris[1] and has also been aired on The Baron, the website featuring news, comment and gossip from Reuters staff, past and present. An editorial urged the newly appointed Editor-in-Chief Alessandra Galloni to refocus on breaking news and warned that the organisation looks alarmingly top heavy at management level when compared to the culling of many experienced journalists in the field (The Baron, 2021a):

> There has been a steady haemorrhaging of senior correspondents and talented juniors around the globe, including Europe and areas of former great strength, like Africa. Some complain of "unbearable pressure" to simultaneously produce both fast breaking news and enterprise stories in under-staffed bureaux, after years of cuts.

One senior Reuters correspondent still with the news agency said the quality of incoming copy from foreign offices was sometimes sub-standard and required thorough rewriting, illustrating the lack of experienced bureau chiefs (who would often oversee important stories before they were sent to an editing desk) or unsustainable pressures of work.

Digging in for the long haul

Foreign news gathering is, of course, just one of the areas in which the profession has been transformed in the past two decades. In an age of social media, news coverage has become image-driven and more emotional, posing fresh challenges to the once dominant objectivity paradigm of Anglo-American media; the combination of social media and polarised politics has seen the emergence of fake news, declining levels of trust in established media and widespread scepticism about the role of journalists in society; and professional ideologies have shifted as journalists are encouraged to develop and promote a personal brand and engage in public debate with audiences in a way that for many had been taboo (Jukes, 2019).

Instinctively, the four major agencies have acted in unison, championing the cause of fact-based news, the value of witnessing and "being there," while trumpeting their expertise in verification. In doing so, they have taken a calculated gamble that the normative values of journalism deeply rooted in their history will in the long-term prevail or, if not prevail, will at least form a trusted counter-weight to opinionated content on social media. That gamble looked ever sounder as the COVID-19 pandemic developed, bringing with it a disturbing new wave of fake news and conspiracy theories. The significant rise in viewing of public service television news during the pandemic (Newman et al., 2021) has played into the hands of the agencies' delivery of wholesale video content as has a shift to trusted brands and reliable, accurate news in the public's consumption habits. But some of the agencies have been able to capitalise on this more than others. As one former Reuters regional editor said:

> The pendulum is going to swing at some stage back to trusted journalism and the question is how do you market that brand of trusted journalism to make sure people realise there is value in it.

Bloomberg's aggressive and slick marketing epitomises the brand potential and confidence of the newcomer, while the other agencies are fighting against the charge that they are "legacy" brands and slower moving. Bloomberg has carefully cultivated its image of cool, from the core client base of market traders who cherish their "Bloomberg" (i.e.

Conclusion 111

terminal) to those who visit its new European headquarters in London. Here, at the base of the spiral stairway ramp or "central vortex," is a new commission by the Icelandic-Danish artist Olafur Eliasson. He is one of six well-known international artists to have been commissioned to create works for the building. Marketing aside, when it comes to news, Bloomberg's strong financial position has enabled it to challenge the previous supremacy of the likes of Reuters and AFP in regions such as the Middle East and Africa. There are signs, however, of a change at Reuters as it adopts a more aggressive branding policy and launches in 2021 a global advertising campaign to position the agency as "The Source," a move that chief marketing officer Josh London says aims to highlight the strength of its reporting (The Baron, 2021b).

> We have an enviable mission with industry-leading reporting," he said. "In many ways, we just have to shine a light on the work we do and let it speak for itself. Up until now, Reuters has tended to be modest as a brand. You could say we are a well-kept secret, operating largely behind the scenes."

Verification has taken on additional significance for both practical and marketing reasons. In practical terms, cuts in foreign news gathering and the dangers of maintaining a presence in conflict zones such as Syria have meant an increased reliance on stringers, freelancers and user-generated content, all of which require careful verification. According to the Committee to Protect Journalists (CPJ), a total of 139 journalists have been killed in Syria since the conflict began in 2011 while the amount of disinformation and misinformation has reached epidemic proportions. From a marketing perspective, the agencies have been able to demonstrate publicly their commitment to fact-based journalism. Both Reuters and AFP have struck deal with Facebook to fact-check content on the platform in various languages around the world. As AFP's Chetwynd observed, the pandemic turned out to be an important opportunity to boost the agency's image as a trustworthy global news provider (2020).

The growing investment in verification, both for the agencies' own news gathering and for third parties, is testimony to their determination to maintain a firm grip on the flow of international news. As Cottle has pointed out, major news organisations have declined to surrender their traditional editorial control, agenda-setting functions or gatekeeper authority when deciding who is permitted to enter "their" news domain, under what conditions, when and how (2009: xi). Attempts to rebalance the global news agenda and weaken the hegemonic grip of the Western news agencies and other major news organisations have only scratched the surface. Online outlets such as *Global Voices* are part of a body of complementary sources of news that do highlight different views but to date their reach is limited. State actors with 24-hour broadcast channels are either poorly funded or are viewed as propaganda machines. The continued dominance of the Western view stems partly from the fact that the global news agencies have recognised the value of social media content and effectively engaged in an act of "colonisation" by packaging it with their own reporting. First-hand testimonies, visceral accounts, and graphic images help to dramatise and humanise stories, injecting emotion and urgency into stories of people's plight and pain (ibid). This is especially true in coverage of conflict and disaster and has an additional benefit for the agencies – it allows them to engage their readers with emotive content without jeopardising their adherence to a fact-based ethos of journalism. Wahl-Jorgensen has pointed out how mainstream news organisations such as agencies are able to uphold their allegiance to journalism's objectivity paradigm by using the technique of "outsourcing" emotion to the protagonists in a story, namely, those who are authorised to express emotions in public and those whose emotions journalists can authoritatively describe without implicating themselves (2013). The ability for agencies to incorporate social media content into news stories adds a further opportunity to employ this technique or "strategic ritual of emotionality," making stories more attractive to wholesale clients or everyday consumers through their public websites.

The pitfalls of social media

At best, the culture of the news agencies and social media make for an awkward mix. The news agencies have on the one hand embraced social media, often with enthusiasm. But on the other hand, in the back of their mind, is the nagging concern that a single tweet could plunge an organisation into crisis and damage public trust at a time of already deep scepticism about established media. They are still uncomfortable being in the public eye, steering a careful course during the most controversial stories of the past few years, not least Brexit, the Trump presidency and COVID-19 pandemic. One careless tweet or social media post can suck an organisation into a veritable storm of polarised and vitriolic comments. Each of the agencies has produced finely tuned social media guidelines for their staff, acknowledging the ubiquity and usefulness of social media tools while at the same time issuing clear warnings that their journalists are entering into previously unknown territory by communicating directly with the public. Agency journalists, who only a generation ago were not used to a byline on their stories, have been swept up in the changing professional ideology that has seen the emergence of media personalities and individual "brands" on social media. It has become routine for journalists to post links to their own stories (and sometimes even those of rivals). Partly this is an act of simple dissemination but it also serves to promote the news organisation in question and the profile of the individual journalist. One AP journalist has already fallen foul of her organisation's social media rules. But arguably the outcry and backlash over the dismissal of Emily Wilder because of allegedly pro-Palestinian views has in itself attracted a wave of negative publicity for AP and achieved the exact opposite of what was intended by its social media policies. After more than 100 AP journalists signed a letter expressing concern over her treatment a review was launched into whether the policies needed overhauling.[2] The agencies are, therefore, in the spotlight like never before, whether they like it or not.

They have also learnt to use social media to their advantage, not least to stand up for press freedom and their own correspondents. Reuters decided to go public and launched an international campaign for the freedom of two of its journalists, Wa Lone and Kyaw Soe Oo after they were jailed in Myanmar in December 2017 for their reporting of the Rohingya crisis. Reuters journalists across the world organised online protests in an attempt to free them in a powerful show of solidarity. On social media platforms #freewalonekyawsoeoo became a viral hashtag, together with photos of solemn Reuters staff in their newsrooms. In one tweet, the whole New York newsroom was photographed standing in rows 10 deep, with journalists holding signs demanding the release of Wa Lone and Kyaw Soe Oo.[3] The two spent more than 500 days in prison before being freed. On their release, the Reuters Editor-in-Chief at the time, Stephen Adler, said the reporters, who had been awarded the Pulitzer prize while still in jail, had become symbols of press freedom. The power and pitfalls of social media are therefore finely balanced in the eyes of the news agencies and pose one of the constant challenges to their editorial practice, business model and, ultimately, their reputation.

Going back to their roots

Slowly but surely, sometimes the hard way, the news agencies have learnt lessons from the past years of tumultuous disruption to the global media landscape. In fighting to stay relevant, they have so far managed to maintain their grip on setting the news agenda and staved off fears that they may no longer have a vital role to play. They may be steeped in more than 150 years of tradition, but none of the major agencies views themselves as an anachronism. On the contrary, there are signs in some of the agencies that confidence is gradually returning after initial soul-searching about their position in the global news ecology.

In returning to their common roots, they have grounded editorial and business strategies in their long track record of providing fact-based news. The fact that all the global agencies have adopted the same stance in the face of the wave of social media opinion, fake news and conspiracy theories bears testimony to the deep-seated common culture that binds together "wire" journalists. It also reflects a generation of editors and news executives who began their careers before the rise of social media and who grew up with the norms of fact-based journalism. This is, however, more than nostalgia for a past era when producing impartial journalism appeared simpler and was not subject to today's intense public scrutiny. It represents a conviction that the agencies have a distinct societal role to play in upholding the democratic function of the media by checking facts, exposing lies and holding power to account.

The strategy around fact-based journalism is both offensive and defensive. The agencies have launched themselves into the task of verifying content for social media platforms, acutely aware that the likes of Facebook and Twitter are under constant pressure to put their houses in order or face regulation. It is a source of new revenue and showcases the agencies' credibility for accurate and truthful news. Sticking to the normative principles of fair and impartial news has also allowed the news agencies to capitalise on the backlash against fake news that has seen organisations such as the *New York Times* rapidly expand their subscription base. It is also a defensive strategy for the agencies, protecting traditional values and firmly marking out their territory in the rapidly changing news landscape. The refusal to cede their role as gatekeepers, or arbiters of what is fit news, is an inherent part of that.

With time, other business opportunities to bolster and expand revenue – needed to support expensive news gathering operations – have emerged. The provision of digital images and video content, both to wholesale and retail markets, is already a key battleground and the comfortable duopoly of APTN and Reuters TV is being challenged by AFP. The image-driven culture of social media, vital to capturing attention and engagement, has made multi-media news products essential. In a similar fashion, Bloomberg and Reuters have identified a potentially large global market for business news that is *not* delivered in real time, second by second, but draws on existing material already produced for the core business aimed at traders in the financial markets. The challenge will be to avoid cannibalising existing revenue streams as financial institutions continue to cut their overheads.

The threats to the news agencies have sometimes been forced on them by the dire financial straits of some of their customers (in the case of AP American newspaper and broadcast members); and sometimes the threats appear to be the result of questionable strategic decisions. Slimming down the network of foreign bureaux may have started out as an unavoidable cost-cutting measure, but the question is whether Reuters and AP have cut too deep, undermined their core news gathering capacity and played into the hands of their competitors. Investing in long-form and lengthy investigative journalism at Reuters has paid dividends in winning Pulitzer prizes and burnished its reputation. But it has also caused deep unease in some parts of the organisation and sparked calls to refocus on breaking news for core customers.

In this difficult media climate, the agencies have tentatively emerged from the shadows. Bloomberg needed no prompting and has continued its brash, confident marketing of its news and brand, epitomised by its new European headquarters in London. But for the others, for more than a century accustomed to keeping a low profile behind the scenes, there are signs they are ready to step up their self-promotion. Slick websites and phrases highlighting their global reach are now standard fare, together with references to the large number of stories and pictures produced (e.g. AP boasts 2,000 stories per day and 1 million photos per year). But in other areas, the agencies display their traditional caution and apprehension about being drawn into the public spotlight. Nowhere is this plainer to see than in the uncomfortable relationship with social media feeds, at once a vital reporting tool and yet a potential risk to reputations should journalists post politically sensitive tweets or retweets.

Some of these changes to the news environment are likely to be long lasting, others are potentially transitory. The shift to visual content and the need to check facts in an unregulated social media environment seem to be well established; it remains to be seen whether the growth in subscriptions to fact-based news outlets will be sustained in a post-pandemic world if the demand for public service-type information recedes. The traditional foreign correspondent has not vanished entirely but certainly the glory days of the expat lifestyle have well and truly disappeared. This has in turn ushered in opportunities for local journalists to work for (and not just with) the international news agencies and may in time lead to the inclusion of more diverse and local voices in mainstream reporting. The one certainty in these uncertain times is that the news agencies face a delicate balancing act as they fight to stay relevant – sticking to the ethos of fact-based journalism while continuing to adapt editorial and business strategies to take account of the ever-shifting media landscape.

Notes

1. See Chapter 2, p. 50.
2. See Chapter 3, p. 73.
3. See: https://twitter.com/williamsmjw/status/1037033098192543744?ref_src=twsrc%5Etfw%7Ctwcamp%5Etweetembed%7Ctwterm%5E1037033098192543744%7Ctwgr%5E%7Ctwcon%5Es1_&ref_url=https%3A%2F%2Fwww.newslaundry.com%2F2018%2F09%2F05%2Ffreewalonekyawsoeoo-in-solidarity-with-jailed-reuters-journalists

References

Agence France-Presse. 2020. Annual report. https://view.afp.com/2020-annual-report/home-page/p/1

Broersma, M. and Graham, T., 2013. Twitter as a news source. How Dutch and British newspapers used tweets in their news coverage, 2007–2011. *Journalism Practice*, 7(4), pp. 446–464.

Cottle, S., 2009. Preface. In Allan, S. and Thorsen, E. (Eds.), *Citizen Journalism: GLOBAL Perspectives* (Vol. 1). New York: Peter Lang.

Di Giovanni, J. 2021. The first draft of history: Why the decline of foreign reporting makes for worse foreign policy. *Foreign Policy*. https://foreignpolicy.com/2021/01/15/history-foreign-correspondents-media-press-journalism-war-reporting-photography/

Jukes, S., 2019. Crossing the line between news and the business of news: Exploring journalists' use of Twitter. *Media and Communication*, 7(1), pp. 248–258.

Kovach, B. 2010. Journalist Bill Kovach about new book "Blur": Journalism verification key to the survival of democracy. http://www.imediaethics.org/News/206/Journalist_bill_kovach_about_new_book_blur___.php

Newman, N., Fletcher, R., Schulz, A., Andi, S., Robertson, C.T. and Nielsen, R.K., 2021. *Reuters institute digital news report 2021*. Oxford: Reuters Institute for the Study of Journalism. https://reutersinstitute.politics.ox.ac.uk/digital-news-report/2021

The Baron, 2021a. Has the penny finally dropped at Reuters? *The Baron*, 16 September 2021. https://www.thebaron.info/editorial/has-the-penny-finally-dropped-at-reuters

The Baron, 2021b. Reuters is The Source – ad. *The Baron*, 27 September 2021. https://thebaron.info/news/article/2021/09/27/reuters-is-the-source-ad

Utley, G., 1997. The shrinking of foreign news: From broadcast to narrowcast. *Foreign Affairs*, 76(2), pp. 2–10.

Wahl-Jorgensen, K., 2013. The strategic ritual of emotionality: A case study of Pulitzer Prize-winning articles. *Journalism*, 14(1), pp. 129–145.

Index

Note: Page references with "n" denotes endnotes.

ABC 76, 106
accidental journalists 63
Adler, Stephen 39, 51, 77, 113
ADN 5
AFP News 49
AFX News 29
Agence France-Presse (AFP) 2, 23, 24–25, 59, 66, 71–72, 74–76, 78, 88, 92, 96–97, 107–109, 111, 114; cuts to editorial 52; digital media 48–49; digital verification network 55; diversity 7; financial news 29–30; financial performance 42, 44; news pictures 33–34; scoops 4–9; video footage 31–32, 49
Agence Havas 15; Agency Alliance Treaty 20; nationalisation of 22
Agency Alliance Treaty 20–21
al-Arabiya 87
al-Assad, Bashar 72, 75, 98
Al-Jazeera 27, 28, 76, 87
Amazeen, M.A. 55, 62, 70
AP-Dow Jones 29–31
APTN 8, 87, 114; video footage 31–32
Arnett, Peter 108
Associated Press (AP) 1, 15, 21, 22, 67, 69, 73–77, 88, 92, 97, 107–109, 113, 115; and Abraham Lincoln assassination report 4; cost cutting 52–53; digital media 48–49; diversity 7; financial difficulties 27–28; financial news 29–30; financial performance 44; news pictures 33–34; overview 2; Pearl Harbor bombing report 5; scoops 4–9; "Wirephoto" operation 33

"bad" journalism 63
Baker, Hazel 65
Baldwin, Clare 51
The Baron 77, 80n12, 92, 109, 111
Barrett, Jane 64, 80n3
Bartram, John 30
Battle of Iwo Jima 33
Bauder, David 73
BBC 54, 61, 63, 76, 85, 87, 96–99, 101
BBC World News 87
BBC World Service Television 87
Berglez, Peter 85, 94
Berlin Wall 5, 6
Bernstein, Carl 89
Black Lives Matter campaign 46
Bloomberg 2, 3, 6, 9, 67, 75, 89, 92, 107, 109–110, 114–115; digital media 46–47; emergence of 29–30; financial customers 30; financial performance 10, 42–43; financial television network 32; revolutionising agency business 30–31; social media 46
Bloomberg, Michael 6, 12n2, 43, 80n14
Bloomberg Business News *see* Bloomberg

Bloomberg by Bloomberg (Bloomberg) 6
Bloomberg News 2, 3, 78
Boaden, Helen 61
Boot, William 3, 12n3
Borges-Rey, E. 90
Boston marathon bombing 68
Botts, Jackie 51
"Boxing Day tsunami" 60, 61, 65, 67
Boyd-Barrett, Oliver 7, 21, 26, 35n10, 36n16
breaking news 2–4; and journalism 3; *see also* news
Breaking News: How the Wheels Came off at Reuters (Mooney and Simpson) 6, 34
Brexit 59, 112
Buell, Hal 33
Bureau Havas 17, 35n1
Bureau of Investigative Journalism 84, 85, 91, 95
Businessweek 39, 51
Buzbee, Sally 53

Cable News Network (CNN) 28, 36n15, 76, 79, 85–87, 97–98, 101, 106
Caribbean News Agency (CANA) 27
carrier pigeons 15
CBS 76
CBS News 76
CCTV America 100
CCTV network 87
Central News Agency 20
Centre for Public Integrity 91
Chamberlain, Neville 22
Chancellor, Christopher 24, 36n13
Chappe, Claude 17
Cherubini, F. 62
Chetwynd, Phil 49, 57n9, 59, 66, 71, 92, 96–97, 109, 111
China Daily 100
China Global Television Network (CGTN) 85, 98, 100–102, 102n1
China Radio International 100
Chirac, Jacques 98
The Christian Science Monitor 76
Chung, Andrew 51
Claypole, Stephen 31
Clinton, Hillary 99
Columbia Journalism Review (CJR) 53, 79, 100
Committee to Protect Journalists (CPJ) 111
community: -based approach 93–97; and international journalism 95–96; and state actors 84–102; volunteer 93
community-oriented journalism 85, 102
competition: for dominance among news agencies 29–34; news agencies 20–21
Cooke, William 17
Cooper, Kent 19–20, 21–22, 33
Cottle, S. 88, 111
"counter hegemonic" networks 85
COVID-19 pandemic 10–11, 34, 56, 59, 64, 65, 91, 110, 112; AFP decrease in earnings 44; news agencies decrease in earnings 41; and newspapers 39
Crimean War 15–16

Dart Centre for Journalism & Trauma 97, 103n13
data journalism 52, 90
Deutsches Nachrichtenbüro 22
Deutsche Welle 98
"digital frontline" 62
digital media 45–49; Agence France-Presse (AFP) 48–49; Associated Press (AP) 48–49; Bloomberg 46–47; Reuters 47; *see also* social media
digital verification network 55
Dowdell, Jaimi 51
Du Preez, Ben 95
Duterte, Rodrigo 51

Eikon 43
Electric Telegraph Company 35n6
Eliasson, Olafur 111
emotional journalism 62
Euronews 87, 98, 101
European Alliance of News Agencies 57n7
Exchange Telegraph 20

Index

Faas, Horst 33
Facebook 55, 65–66, 74, 80n4, 106–107, 111, 114
fact-based journalism 59–60, 63, 67, 79, 86, 107, 111, 114, 116
fact-checking: in practice 64–67; taking on new dimensions 60–64
Factcheck.org 55, 58n13, 62
fake news 7, 54–55, 66, 70, 76, 79, 100, 110, 114
Fauci, Anthony 66
Financial Times 4, 6, 34, 42, 46, 52
Fitzgibbon, Will 90
Foreign Affairs 106
Fox News 63, 79, 87
France-24 87, 98, 101
Franco-Austrian war 19
Franco-Prussian war 16
Freeman, Colin 4
free speech 93
Fries, Fabrice 32
Future News Worldwide 80n3

Galloni, Alessandra 7, 9, 92, 109
gatekeepers 12, 67, 69, 107, 114; *de facto* 78; elite 70; traditional 102
gatekeeping 60, 70, 101; defined 80n8; or "gatewatching" 67–72
"gatewatching" 67–72
GB News 63
Gellhorn, Martha 89
general news 9
Getty Images 33–34, 48
Giovanni, Janine di 108
The Globalisation of News (Boyd-Barrett and Rantanen) 7
global journalism 94
Global Voices 85, 93–94, 97, 101, 112
Glocer, Tom 43
Gobright, Lawrence 4
Goldman Sachs 42
Graves, L. 62
Griessner, M.C. 60, 73
The Guardian newspaper 43, 69, 72
Gulf War 98
Gyllenhammar, Pehr 24, 36n12

Hachten, William 6
Hajj, Adnan 75
"hard news" stories 16

Havas, Charles-Louis 15, 17, 20, 35n1, 88
Himmler, Heinrich 22
Hitler, Adolf 89
Holland, Steve 77
Honecker, Erich 5
Hoog, Emmanuel 8
HSBC 42
Hudson, Michael 90
Hurley, Lawrence 51
Huteau, Jean 6, 23, 27

imperialism, and news agencies 26–27
Indian Ocean earthquake 60, 61, 65, 67
Instagram 55, 80n4, 106
Institute for War & Peace Reporting (IWPR) 93–95, 101
International Consortium of Investigative Journalists (ICIJ) 85, 90–91, 101
International Fact-Checking Network 67
International Journalism (Williams) 6
investigative journalism 92, 115

Januta, Andrea 51
Johnson, Boris 69
Jones, Roderick 22
journalism 1; "bad" 63; and breaking news 3; community-oriented 85, 102; data 52, 90; emotional 62; fact-based 18, 20, 40, 59–60, 67, 79, 86, 107, 111, 114, 116; global 94; investigative 92, 115; news agency 10; parachute 94–96; plain vanilla 10, 11, 17, 35, 40, 54, 59–80, 95, 101; "shock jock" 87; Western-style of 21
journalists: accidental 63; as naïve empiricists 18; parachute 5, 93, 94, 95, 96, 103n10

Kurdi, Alan 96

Le Monde 50, 109
Leridon, Michele 7–8
Lewis, C. 90

Lincoln, Abraham 4
Lippmann, Walter 19
London, Josh 47, 111
London bombings 60–61, 65, 67
London Stock Exchange 43
Lone, Wa 51, 113
Long, Gerald 27
Lutyens, Sir Edwin 12n1

MacBride, Sean 26–27
MacBride Report 26–27
Macdowall, Ian 25–26
MacKinnon, Rebecca 93
MailOnline 68
Marshall, Andrew 51
Mason, Jeff 77
McCullin, Don 108
Media: An Introduction 7
media imperialism 35n10
Mélamed, Georges 33
Mexican-American war 88
Micklethwait, John 52, 78
Mitchell, Austin 28
Mogato, Manuel 51
Mooney, Brian 6, 34
moral injury 103n12
Mossack Fonseca 90
MSNBC 87
Murdoch, Rupert 29, 87

Nasser, Gamal Abdel 24
NBC 76, 106
news: fake 7, 54–55, 66, 70, 76, 79, 100, 110, 114; plain vanilla 10, 11, 17, 35, 40, 54, 59–80, 95, 101; values and norms 18–20
News Corporation 87
News International 29
Newspaper Proprietors Association 23
news pictures 33–34
New York Times 4, 46, 54, 63, 76, 77, 79, 91, 109, 114
normative values 9–10

objectivity 2, 9, 10, 11, 18, 19, 25, 39, 60, 61, 63, 64, 71, 73, 86, 97, 98, 110, 112
Ofcom 68, 99–100

Office Français d'Information (OFI) 22
Oo, Kyaw Soe 51, 113

Pace, Julie 7, 9, 32
Palat, Robert 33
Palmer, Michael 3, 18, 20, 22, 23, 33, 36n16
pan-African agencies (PANA) 27
Panama Papers 11, 84, 90, 101
Pandora Papers 11, 84, 101, 103n17
parachute journalism 5, 93, 94–96, 103n10
Paradise Papers 11, 84, 90, 101
Pearl Harbor bombing 5
People's Daily 100
Phuc, Kim 13n9, 33
Pigeat, Henri 27
pitfalls of social media 112–113
plain vanilla journalism 10, 11, 17, 35, 40, 54, 59–80, 95, 101
Pope John Paul II 5
post-traumatic stress disorder (PTSD) 97, 103n14
The Power of News (Read) 6
Poynter Institute for Media Studies 52, 67, 80n6
Press Association 23
Press TV 87, 98, 100
Pulitzer, Joseph 19

Rahmani, Noorrahman 95
Raimbaud, André 33
Rantanen, Terhi 7, 36n16
Read, Donald 6, 16, 19, 20, 21, 22, 24, 27, 33, 35n3
Reuter, Paul Julius 17, 18, 19
Reuters 1–2, 3, 23–24, 65, 72, 74–77, 88–92, 97, 107–111, 113–115; Agency Alliance Treaty 7; Cooper's criticism of 21–22; cuts to editorial 50; digital media 47; diversity 7; financial difficulties 28, 34; financial news 29–30; financial performance 10, 42–43; investigative journalism, investing in 51; news pictures 33–34; raising capital by public flotation 28–29; scoops 4–9; social media guidelines 74

Reuters.com 76
Reuters Financial TV (RFTV) 31
Reuters Founders Share Company 24, 35n11
Reuters Institute for the Study of Journalism 41, 46, 48, 54, 56, 63–64, 110
Reuters News 12n8, 43–44
Reuters Trust principles 2, 23, 24, 28, 36n14, 39, 77
Reuters TV 49, 87, 114
Rosenthal, Joe 33
RT 85, 94, 98–99, 101–102, 102n2
RT America 99
Russell, William Howard 15–16, 35n2
Russia Today *see* RT

Sambrook, Richard 4, 68
Scoop (Waugh) 3
scoops: AFP 4–9; AP 4–9; Reuters 4–9
Scotton, James F. 6
Scrolling News: The Changing Face of News Consumption report 68
Shah of Iran 5
"shock jock" journalism 87
Short, George 2
Sigal, Ivan 94
Simpson, Barry 6, 34
Singer, J. 61
Skripal, Sergei 99, 102, 103n16
Skripal, Yulia 99, 102
Sky News Arabia 76
Smith, James 43
Snowden, Edward 90
social media 45–49; Agence France-Presse (AFP) 48–49; Associated Press (AP) 48–49; Bloomberg 46; mindset 68; pitfalls of 112–113; Reuters 47; *see also* digital media
Société Générale 42
Stalin, Josef 5
state actors 84–102; with 24-hour broadcast channels 112
A Stricken Field (Gellhorn) 89
Süddeutsche Zeitung 90
Suez crisis 24, 25
Sultana, Zarah 96
Sunday Times 108

Syrian Civil Defence Force 72
Syrian conflict 71, 75, 94, 96, 98, 108
Syrian Electronic Army 75
Szep, Jason 51
Szlukovenyi, Tom 75

taboo and collaboration 88–92
Taliban 69, 95
"Telegrafenstil" 19
Telerate 28
Thomson Corporation 6, 34
Thomson Reuters Corporation 12n8, 23, 24, 42, 43, 44, 50
Thussu, D.K. 87
TikTok 55
The Times 16
Trump, Donald 54, 59, 112; covering 76–78
Trust Principles 2, 23, 24, 28, 36n14, 39, 77
Twitter 11, 48, 57, 60, 63, 64, 72, 74, 75, 76, 79, 106, 114
"Twitter storm" 64
2021 Digital News Report 41, 46, 48, 54, 56, 63–64, 110

Ullmann, Bernard 6, 23, 27
United Nations Educational, Scientific and Cultural Organisation (UNESCO) 26–27, 87
United Press 21, 22–23, 35n9; financial difficulties 27–28
user-generated content 61, 64–65, 67–69, 72, 78, 106, 111
Ut, Nick 6, 13n9
Utley, Garrick 106, 108

video footage: Agence France-Presse (AFP) 31–32, 49; APTN 31–32; Reuters 31–32
Vietnam War 108
Vignal, Patrick 50
Visnews 31

Wahl, Liz 99
Wahl-Jorgensen, Karin 10, 26, 68, 112
Wall Street Journal 39, 51
Washington Post 12n4, 25, 76, 89
Waugh, Evelyn 3

Wheatstone, Charles 17
White, David Manning 70
White Helmets 72
Widener, Jeff 6
Wilder, Emily 73, 113
Williams, Kevin 4, 6, 16, 17, 20, 21, 23, 27, 86
Winkler, Matthew 6, 30
"wire copy" 19
Wolff 17, 20, 21–22, 88
Wolff, Bernhard 17, 20
Wolff's Telegraphisches Bureau 15
Wood, Mark 47, 79

Woodward, Bob 89
The World News Prism: Challenges of Digital Communication (Hachten and Scotton) 6
World War II 2, 4, 22, 33
Worldwide Television News 31

Xinhua 100

Yates, Dean 97, 103n15
YouGov 80n2

Zuckerman, Ethan 93